DEAN

More KIDS SPEAK

Children Talk About Themselves

by Chaim Walder

translated by Shifra Slater

Illustrated by Yoni Gerstein

FELDHEIM
Jerusalem □ New York

Originally published in 1994 in Hebrew
as *Yeladim Mesaprim al Atzmam* (Vol. 2)

First published 1995
ISBN 0-87306-720-7

FELDHEIM PUBLISHERS
POB 35002 / Jerusalem, Israel

200 Airport Executive Park
Nanuet, NY 10954

10 9 8 7 6 5 4 3 2 1

typeset at Astronel, Jerusalem

Printed in Israel

Approbation for Volume One from **Rabbi Yitzchak Silberstein**, *shlita*

הנושא של חינוך הילדים, לתורה, ויר"ש ומדות טובות, תופס מקום בראש, של כל יהודי, ומלאכת החינוך דורשת עיון. מחשבה ותושיה, ועל כולם תפילה בכל לב להשי"ת. הרב חיים ולדר שליט"א בתור מחנך, בא לעזור להורים בעצה וחכמה כיצד לעזור לילדיהם להתגבר על בעיות המפריעות להם. הבה ונחזיק לו טובה על כך.

דכירנא, בלומדנו בישיבת סלבודקה, בא תלמיד לפני ראש הישיבה הגה"צ ר' אייזיק שר זצ"ל וסיפר לו על חברו בחדר האוכל שמשוחח כל היום על רכישת מעלות חמריות, וממון, ושאל את ראש הישיבה כיצד להתגבר על כך, שלא יושפע מחבירו? וגם ביקש להרחיק את החבר משכנותו!

כנראה שראש הישיבה זצ"ל ראה בדברי בחור זה, קצת יהירות, אמר לו: החובת לבבות מודה להשי"ת על כל טובותיו, שגמל עמו ואחד מהם היא שמחשבותיו נסתרות ואין איש יודע ומכירם, אחרת היו חבריו בורחים ממנו...., אם היו יודעים מחשבותיו! אם אתה גם היית חושב כך, היית דואג על נגעי לבבך, ולא היית שם לב לנגעי חברך.

והשי"ת יעזרנו ללמוד וללמד לעשות הישר בעיניו   **יצחק זילברשטיין**

Approbation for Volume One from **Rabbi Avraham Gombo**, *shlita*

להר"ר חיים ולדר שיחי'

ראיתי את ספרך היפה והחינוכי והיתה לי זו שעה של קורת רוח ושמחה ואכן ראויים הדברים למי שכותבם.

שהרי העיקר בעבודתינו החינוכית היא הקניית הרגלי חשיבה נכונים ומידות טובות לתלמידים ובפרט בהנהגות שבין תלמיד לרעהו.

ואישיות כמוך המכיר את נפש הילד והנמצא עמהם בבעיותיהם התמידיות יודֵע יפה כיצד להביע בכתב את קשייהם לבטיהם ופתרונותיהם כאחד בבעיות היום יום של ה"בין אדם לחבירו".

יה"ר וחפץ ד' בידך יצליח, ודפי הספר יפיקו את התועלת הנכספת, והיא לבנות תלמידים צעירי הצאן הבנים במידות טובות ובדרך ארץ שהם מקניני התורה הקדושה.

בברכה והערכה   **אברהם ישראל גומבו**

תלמוד תורה
דקהלת
"משכנות יעקב"

רח' אמרי ח"ם 28
בני-ברק
טל. 03-6743328

בס"ד

תאריך אבן לסדר אחר שלא יבא אל הקדש (ויקרא ט"ז)

לכבוד הרב ח"מ נלבר שליט"א

כקבלתי עברית על רוב דפי הספורים בספרק, לברי נוספים של שלמה
הלק הן וכדגמי שלד. עפ"י עיוני אמנים אותק הגדלתתך בכמה, כאולדן שונק
ירדו של הילר ואיו אין גישלו ואנול על פתרון בכצלתו של, וכדן אלדם לחריו,
הצבית הלק ענב ררק הספר של הלבה, להדי, יונק ירדה לשלים
בבצ'ל ולבצירי אך להם ו אינם מרעלים שיש לדם של ש לבולי או להביר
אית הכצ'יה. וכדי לעונן ספר הכבאב פתרונת לגלא הלקהים אישלא
בינון של הלד ו לאור לקח מן האבאל כלוקת חולת, וגבורה בכזב
להחבירם אלד ו נכצר לשמון לדוי ושמנים. והבצלה,
ספר קראם חולן בצורה שנב ושגני בב עם קבצה אישלא.

ואוים לקאן כבל יל.

בידידות ובהערכה
יצחק כריד

*With gratitude and appreciation, this book is
dedicated to all those children who shared
their experiences and their feelings with me,
thereby opening a window onto a very special
world — the world of children.*

To My Young Readers

There are many, many children in the world — and each and every one of you *is* an entire world.

Everybody has moments of joy and moments of sadness, of tears and of laughter. Each of you can think of things that frighten you or make you worry, and things that make you feel good inside. And yet, even though your own life is different from any other child's, there *are* things which you all have in common. And if you realize that, you can learn how to deal with problems which you might have thought only you have.

In my first book, I told you that if any of you would like to write to me, I would be very happy to hear from you. How wonderful it was to receive thousands of delightful letters!

From your stories, children — the sad ones and the happy ones, the funny ones and the serious ones — this book was born.

I want to thank you all, and to tell you once again that as a teacher of children around your age, I know that a problem can find its solution only if you are able to talk about it. Because if you keep it a secret, the problem will remain inside your heart and might grow so big that you can't bear it.

Most of the time, your mother or father, your teacher, or even a friend, will be able to help you solve your problem. But first, you must tell them what's troubling you.

If any of you would like to write to me, I will be happy to receive your letters. You can write to: KIDS SPEAK, P.O.B. 211, Bnei Brak, Israel. With Hashem's help, I will answer you.

Happy reading!

Chaim Walder

Contents

The Fire Spy *by Rami*   11

Bittersweet Chocolate *by Judy*   18

A Little Nighttime Problem *by Shaya*   24

Gifts of Love *by Micha'el*   27

For No Good Reason *by Blumie*   34

A Dangerous Game *by Yechezkel*   41

My Special Brother *by Shira*   51

The Boom Boom Man *by Ariel*   57

There's Hope *by Avi*   65

Freddy *by Ilana*   70

The Pressure Cooker *by Menasheh*   77

You're Right! *by Baily*   83

It Must Be Angels *by Ezra*   86

The Hill Battle *by Moishy*   95

When Bad Luck is Good Luck *by Chaya*   105

World's Most Miserable Champ *by Aharon*   112

Alone *by Tammy*   119

Identical and Different *by Gadi*   125

The Fib *by Tzippy*   132

Metal Mouth *by Yanky*   138

Very Funny, But... *by Nechama*   146

Latchkey Kid *by Meir*   149

Thanks to a Strict Teacher *by Sara*   155

My Kid B(r)other *by Mordechai*   164

On Being Nice *by Tali*   169

The Pilot *by Rafi*   176

I Can Do It *by Mindy*   180

Why Can't I Read? *by Gershon*   186

My Father's Tractor *by Dina*   191

Friends Who Argue *by Aryeh*   197

Glossary   203

The Fire Spy

My name is Rami. I'm ten and a half, and I live in Bnei Brak. I always used to build a bonfire on Lag Ba-Omer — every year. Why do I say "used to"? Let me tell you the story.

In my neighborhood, we don't just have one big bonfire for everybody on Lag Ba-Omer. Each group of kids builds its own.

Mine was always called "Rami's fire" and there was another one — sort of competing with mine — called "Shaike's fire." You see, both Shaike and I really know how to get a good fire going, so we were always the ones in charge.

Anyway, around three weeks before Lag Ba-Omer every year, you could see giant piles of wood growing even bigger in two different spots in the neighborhood. Each group would race the other group and argue over who had collected more wood. I mean, if one group managed to get hold of an old door that someone had thrown away, the other group knew it had lost the battle.

It was a real competition — almost a war. And just like in real war, we had to be on the lookout for spies...

Before last Lag Ba-Omer, I had told Uri at recess that I had seen some boards thrown into the garbage behind a nearby building, and we arranged to go get them after school. I didn't notice that Reuven — one of Shaike's group — happened to be standing near us. After school, we went to the building, but just as we arrived, we saw some kids from Shaike's group walking off with the boards!

One day, while we were standing near our pile of wood, trying to figure out where to look for more, I suddenly realized that Shmulik was hanging around with us. Shmulik lives in our neighborhood, but he never was a part of "my" gang.

"What are you doing here?" I asked him.

"Just l-looking..." he mumbled, with a shrug.

"What for?" I asked him, angry. "So you can spy on us and tell Shaike what we're planning?"

"No way!" Shmulik said, "I'm not a spy!"

"He is too," snapped Uri. "I saw him hanging around Shaike's pile the other day."

"Is that true?" I asked Shmulik.

"Yes, but…" Shmulik began, uncomfortable.

"No buts!" I said sharply. "Get away from here, and don't you dare come back!" Shmulik turned and walked away, hurt and ashamed.

I slapped Uri approvingly on the back. "Our counterspy system is really working!" I said, proud of myself.

The days passed and the piles of wood grew higher and higher. We put together a giant, stuffed Haman doll to burn, and hid it in my house so that Shaike's group wouldn't see how big it was and make theirs even bigger.

And then came the big day. Lag Ba-Omer!

At eight o'clock I lit our bonfire. At the same time, just a few yards away, Shaike lit his bonfire.

Naturally, each group of boys looked at the other's fire and said theirs was bigger, better and would burn longer…and each group thought their Haman doll was the best.

I looked at the other bonfire and at ours, and I felt really good. But then, all of a sudden, I had a thought.

I walked over to Shaike's fire. All his friends watched me, and someone asked, "Looking for something?" I was, but I didn't find what I was looking for.

Shaike asked, kind of making fun, "What is it you're looking for, exactly?"

"I'm looking for Shmulik," I answered.

"Shmulik?" Shaike was surprised. "Shmulik's your spy. What would he be doing here?"

"My spy?" I was shocked. "But I chased him away — I thought he was spying for you."

Shaike's tone changed, and he was serious now. "I also chased him away — for the same reason."

We both stood there, troubled, and one by one all the boys came over and gathered around the two of us.

"I'm going to look for Shmulik," I said, and I started to walk off.

"Wait a minute," said someone. "I'm going with you." It was Shaike.

We left the others to keep an eye on the fires, and without a word, we walked towards Shmulik's house. When we got there, we stopped for a minute and looked at each other. Then we both tapped lightly on the door. His mother answered.

"Is Shmulik home?" I asked.

"He went to the bonfire," she said.

"He wasn't at my fire," I said.

"He wasn't at mine either," added Shaike.

Now his mother looked alarmed. "But where could he be?"

"Is it possible he's still in his room?" I asked.

We all walked to the door of Shmulik's room.

His mother opened it, and there was Shmulik. He was all alone in the dark, his head resting on his hands, which were folded on top of his desk.

"Shmulik!" I called to him, "It's me — Rami."

Shmulik didn't budge.

"I'm here, too," added Shaike. "We came to get you. We want you to come with us to the bonfires."

Shmulik lifted his head, and looked up at us, not believing his ears. His eyes were filled with tears. I could see that he was surprised, even though he didn't say a word.

I spoke first. "Shmulik, I'm really sorry. I feel terrible that I said you were spying for Shaike."

"I also want to apologize," said Shaike. "We both messed up."

Shmulik still didn't say a word and he didn't move from his desk.

"Please come," I begged him.

Shmulik stood up and looked at his mother, who also had tears in her eyes. He said, "Sure, I'll come to the bonfires." He picked up the bag of potatoes his mother had prepared, and followed us out the door.

As we got closer to the field, and we saw the fires lighting up the sky, Shmulik asked, "Whose fire do I go to?"

"Mine," we both answered at the same time.

Shmulik looked from Shaike to me and back again. Boy, was he confused!

Shaike and I looked at each other. "Say, don't you think one big bonfire would be better than two?" I asked.

"Sure," answered Shaike. "Who needs two? I thought of it last year, but I was afraid you would say no."

"Well now I say yes!" I said. "And how!"

All of a sudden, a thunder-like sound broke out all around us. The boys from both fires had gathered around, and all of them were applauding.

So that's it, kids. This coming year there's just one bonfire. When you think about it, it really was ridiculous. What a shame that on Lag Ba-Omer, of all days — the day we're supposed to learn about love among friends, the day when the plague that killed Rabbi Akiva's students stopped — we should be fighting and suspicious of each other! What for?

Bittersweet Chocolate

My name is Judy.

I'm writing this letter in bed. It's eight o'clock at night, and I'm alone in my room. I'm really nervous.

An hour ago, my parents went to a parent–teachers meeting at my school. They left with smiles on their faces, and my father said, "We're off to school to fill up our pockets with *nachas*." He pinched my cheek and walked out the door.

Oh boy. I've been sitting here since then, with my heart beating so loud I can hear it! I am really scared. Do you want to know why? Because my parents are not going to come back smiling. They are not going to be happy at all. They'll be angry, and my father will probably punish me. They won't be hearing any good news. Far from it!

You must be wondering why they went out

with such high hopes. I'll tell you. Until recently, I was considered a really good student. I used to get high marks on tests, I did all my homework, my handwriting was neat, and my report cards were really good.

Every time there was a parent–teachers meeting, my parents would come home beaming. My father liked to take out his little note pad and read me all the good things he had heard and jotted down. My mother would add some things of her own. And then, they would present me with the treat they had selected for me on their way home. I always felt so good.

But this time, I dread the "present" they're going to bring me. Even worse — I dread how disappointed they'll be!

They're going to hear some really bad things. You see, a few months ago I stopped being a good student. My homework, when I did it at all, was half-done, and sloppy. And the marks I've been getting on tests — it's hard to believe they're mine. In class, I just sit and dream... The teacher keeps calling me to her desk to ask me what's wrong.

But I never have an answer for her...because I don't *know* what's wrong. Truth is, I never gave it much thought. Maybe I should have talked it over with my parents. Maybe they would have had an idea for me. But now it's too late...

At this very moment, my parents are hearing the awful truth. No...wait...I think I hear them opening the door. Yes! Uh-oh, I'll write more later.

Whew. *Baruch Hashem*, it's all over. About an hour ago, my parents knocked lightly on my door. I opened it, scared and shaking. My father looked at my face for a minute and then he said, "You must be waiting for your treat. Here it is." He put his hand into his pocket and took out a chocolate bar. He handed it to me and then he and my mother started to walk out!

I ran after them. "Wait, don't go. Talk to me; don't just walk away."

"You got your treat," said my father. "What else do you want?"

"The note pad," I said, even though I couldn't look him in the eye because I was so ashamed. "I want to know what the teachers told you."

"I'm sure you already know everything that's written there," said my mother. But they both came back into my room.

Very quietly, my father read me what he'd been told. It was just as I expected.

When he finished, he flipped the note pad shut and looked at me expectantly. They both seemed mad...and sad.

My mother spoke first. "Judy," she said, "It's

not the low marks. Of course, we're not thrilled about them, but we're not angry. What makes us angry is the fact that we had to hear about them from your teacher instead of from you, and that it's been going on for quite a while!"

"I was afraid to tell you about it," I said.

"Afraid? What do you think we would have done to you if you'd come to us and told us that you were having trouble studying, or that you'd started getting lower marks? Do you think we would have yelled at you?" my father asked.

I didn't know, so I kept quiet.

"Don't you think we would have tried to help you?" my mother added.

I still kept quiet. Of course they were right.

My mother came over to my bed and gave me the tightest hug. Suddenly, I felt so warm and good and loved. I felt as if she had just given me the strength to turn around the whole train that was taking me away from doing well in school. I felt I could get back on track and start working the way I used to.

Then my father told me about the time the same thing had happened to him in school. He told me that almost everyone goes through a time like that, when he can't seem to do well in school. He had some ideas on how I could change certain things.

He and my mother kept reminding me that

doing poorly in school would never make them mad. But the fact that I didn't talk to them about it and ask for their help was another story. Finally, my parents made a plan with me for helping me study and do my homework. Before they left the room, they each gave me a kiss.

My father was at the door when I suddenly said, "Abba!"

He turned around.

"W-w-why did you buy me chocolate?" I asked.

My father laughed. "We bought you chocolate because we love you," he answered.

"But you heard such bad things about me, and you were angry that I didn't tell you, so I didn't really deserve it."

"Well," said my mother as she poked her head back into my room, "the truth is we thought about it, and chose something to let you know our feelings. Take a closer look at the chocolate bar."

They left and closed the door. I took the chocolate out of its little paper bag, and then I smiled. The chocolate was bittersweet.

Dear Chaim Walder,

I read your book <u>Kids Speak</u>, and I decided to tell my story, and not to keep quiet anymore.

Yours truly,
And I hope you take my story,
David.

My name is David.

I am in the sixth grade. There are nine kids in my family – b'li <u>ayin hara</u>, <u>ken yirbu</u> – four older than me, four younger than me. I'm in the middle – I'm what they call the sandwich. I know other sandwiches, and a lot of them say it's good to be in the middle because you have all the advantages of the big ones, and all the advantages of the little ones. But I don't find that. I find that I get all the problems of the older ones, and then all the problems of the younger ones! They consider me one of the younger ones now anyway, because all my older brothers are Bar Mitzvah already and I'm just ten and a half and every time I complain that I'm not one of the younger ones anymore, they just laugh and say, "You're the spread inside the sandwich, so you're bound to get smooshed." Or they say, "You may not be little anymore, but you're not big yet either." Or, if I ask for some sweet, they laugh and remind me that I'm the spread inside the sandwich and I'm sweet enough! And then, when I asked for a Walkman for an <u>afikoman</u> present, they told me I should let the littler kids have the prizes instead. (All of a sudden, they decided I was big enough to give in, and let the "little ones" have their way, but if I ever want to be considered big, forget it!) Another example: Our sukkah walls are stored up on a high balcony that doesn't have such a high railing, and no one's allowed to go up there except my big brothers before sukkos, to bring them down. So this year I asked if I could go up with them and my parents said, "No, you're still little". Pesach, they also let my big brothers go up to the storage area and take down the cartons of Pesach dishes. (In our family, the best thing ever is to go up and get those cartons down) So I really don't think it's worth it being the sandwich.

A Little
Nighttime Problem

My name is Shaya. I'm eight and I'm in the third grade. I'm going to tell you about my problem, even though it's awfully embarrassing. Other people have the same problem, but they usually don't talk about it. But I decided that I really need to get it off my chest.

You see, my problem has to do with sleeping. I sleep very soundly — you might even say too soundly. A bulldozer plowing through my bedroom wouldn't wake me up!

You're probably wondering, "So what's so bad about being a sound sleeper?" Um...well, the problem is that when I do wake up, I'm soaking wet.

When I was little, my mother didn't make a big deal about it. But by the time I reached first grade and then second, she started asking me gently if I didn't think it was time to start controlling myself. Then, slowly, she and I started to realize that I had a certain problem, and that we would have to take care of it.

At first, my mother tried waking me up in the middle of the night. But that didn't help. Then she took me to somebody who was supposed to be an expert in helping kids with this problem. He gave me pills, but they didn't help, either.

Every time I wake up in the morning, I feel just awful. Then, when I go to school, I'm always afraid my friends will somehow find out.

When a friend invites me to sleep over, I always have to make up some excuse why I can't go. I'm even too embarrassed to sleep over at my cousin's house. My brothers and sisters sleep at their friends' houses — they don't have this problem — and when they come home they talk and talk about all the fun they had. I feel like my heart is going to break. I am missing out on so much!

I tried very hard to stop my problem. I followed every method my mother ever heard about. Nothing worked; everyone said I would just grow out of it some time.

Then one day I couldn't take it anymore. I cried to my mother, "I'll never grow out of this. I'll be this way my whole life! Do something!"

"Well," she replied, stroking my hair, "There

is one more expert I was thinking of taking you to..."

This expert was different. She listened to my whole story and said, "Don't think it's because you're not trying hard enough. Nowadays we think this problem comes from the fact that the bridge between the brain and the muscles is not strong enough. What you need are some sports to help you work your left side and your right side more."

Guess what she prescribed! No, it wasn't any medicine. She told me to take karate lessons and to practice running and pumping my arms at the same time. What a fun cure!

I really don't want to make this story too long. I just want to tell you that at first the karate and running were a little hard for me. I couldn't get my body to do what I wanted when I wanted. But I didn't give up, and I'm happy to say: Nighttime isn't a problem anymore.

Gifts of Love

My name is Micha'el. I'm in the fourth grade, and I'm considered a pretty good kid.

I have the oldest book bag in the class. I got it from my older brother, and he got it from our oldest brother.

Our parents don't have much money, so I guess you'd call us poor. Sometimes they tell us stories in school about poor people. I look around at the other kids then, and I can see that they think these things really don't happen anymore. But for me and for my brothers, the stories are about what happens in our house every day.

From what the teachers say, though, it always seems like poor people are unhappy. I used to think that too...until I realized that *we* were poor.

Once when I spoke to my father about it, he reminded me that it says in *Pirkei Avos*: "Who is

rich? The one who is happy with what he has."
He told me that there are some people who have
a lot of money but are very sad — maybe because
nobody likes them, or maybe because of other
things.

"Love and happiness are things that money
can't buy," my father said.

And I can see it's true, because in our house
there's lots of love — even though there's very
little money.

My father is so proud of me. He always says,
"I don't care if I never have money, as long as I
always have a son who learns so well!" I try very
hard all the time to make him proud, so that
he can always be happy with what he has and
always be "rich."

A few days ago, it was my father's birthday.
Fathers don't celebrate birthdays much, especially a father like mine, who's really serious and
who doesn't have much money. But I decided
anyway to buy my father a present.

My father has this old-fashioned fountain
pen, that he keeps in his desk. A fountain pen
is a strange kind of pen — it looks like a quill or
something that a *sofer* uses. It doesn't have a
refill or a cartridge or anything like new fountain
pens do. Instead, you have to dip it into this little
jar filled with ink that's very expensive. Just like
in the old days.

My father is a writer. He writes *chiddushim*, new ideas explaining parts of the Torah, all the time. He used to love writing with that fountain pen, but the ink cost too much, so now the fountain pen sits in its box in the top drawer of his desk. My father writes with an ordinary pen, like everybody else.

Well, I decided I would buy my father a jar of that special ink. I knew it would make him very happy. But I didn't have the money for it.

I looked through my things to see if there was something I could sell, but pretty soon I realized that I didn't own anything that anybody would be willing to pay for. All my stuff is pretty worn out...

Then all of a sudden I remembered my new pocket calculator. I had won it in school last week for getting the highest grades in math of all my classmates. I hadn't used it yet, though, because it came without batteries. I didn't have any money of my own to buy them with, and I didn't want to ask my parents for the money and put them on the spot. So I *did* own something of value!

I went to the stationery store, and I showed the calculator, new in its package, to the store-keeper. "Could you exchange this for a jar of ink?" I asked him, showing him the kind of ink I wanted.

The storekeeper smiled. He wrote down their prices and did some figuring, and then he gave me seven jars!

I went home very happy. Now my father would have enough ink for two years. He was going to be so happy with my gift!

I wasn't even a little sad about giving up the calculator. I love my father more than anything. Besides, what good was the calculator to me? I didn't even know how to use it.

I got home with my package, which the store-keeper had gift-wrapped for me, and I waited impatiently for my father to come home.

But he came home later than usual, and as soon as he walked in, he said, "Micha'el, let me see your calculator."

"My calculator?" I was stunned. "It–it's not…here," I stammered.

"Not here?" asked my father, alarmed. "What happened to it?"

I couldn't tell him.

"Micha'el, answer me!"

"I–I s-sold it, Abba," I answered quietly.

"You *sold* it?" my father asked, alarmed. "Why?"

"I sold it because I wanted to buy you a birthday present," I confessed.

My father's face was turning pale. "Abba," I cried, "what's wrong?"

My father didn't answer. Instead, he slowly took a package out of his pocket and handed it to me. "I wanted to buy you a present, because you've been learning so well," he said.

I opened up the wrapping paper, and then I understood. Inside was a set of batteries for my new calculator. The one I had sold.

We were both silent. Then I said, "Oh, it doesn't matter, Abba. Now open the present I bought for you."

My father opened the package and looked at the seven jars of ink in amazement. And then he let out a sigh that broke my heart.

"Abba, what is it?" I asked. "What's wrong?"

"My dear son," said my father, pulling me towards him, "you bought me the special ink for my fountain pen. But just today, I sold it to get the money to buy you a gift."

For a very long time I stood still, in my father's arms. We held each other very tight. I didn't dare look into his face. Finally, I peered up at him, and I saw that he was smiling.

"Micha'el," said my father, "do you know why people buy presents for each other?"

"To show their love," I answered him.

"You just gave me the best present in the whole wide world," my father said. He pointed to the ink jars on the table, the jars that now had no purpose, and continued, "I can't think

of any better thing to buy that would so clearly show your love for me than these."

And do you know what? At that moment, I had the best feeling — I was the richest and most loved boy of all, who had the most wonderful father there ever could be.

Those batteries were the best present I'd ever received in my whole life. And that was the happiest birthday for my father, too.

For No Good Reason

My name is Blumie. I'm in the sixth grade. I'm a pretty sociable girl, but I tend to be a little too sensitive.

Up until this year, I used to go to a different school, near my house. But this year, I switched to a new one, further away.

Why did I switch? Well, the other school just wasn't right for me. Don't think it wasn't a good school. That's not it at all. In fact, it's considered to be one of the best. But it just wasn't the place for me. That's how I felt, and my parents felt the same way.

At first, I was afraid of the change, especially the social part. I didn't know if the kids in the new school would act friendly to me. But what a relief! The girls accepted me right away. They took me in and acted as if I had been their classmate since the first grade.

My problem came from somewhere else —

and it was something I never would have expected. It involved the girls from my old school!

Two weeks into the school year, I was passing
my old schoolyard — the school is near my
house, remember? — when I thought I heard
my name. I looked toward the fence and I saw
a lot of girls standing together and looking at
me. Mostly, they were from the class below me.
They were whispering — but not so quietly that
I couldn't hear!

"That's Blumie, remember her?"

"Sure, Blumie from the fifth grade."

"She was in Etti's class."

"She switched schools."

"Yeah, she couldn't make it here."

I blushed, and started to walk faster. I
wanted to get away from there as fast as possible. But the girls walked out of the schoolyard
and looked after me, their whispering getting
louder and louder.

I can't exactly explain how I felt. I was kind
of afraid, though I don't know why. I mean, they
didn't do anything to me. But I felt hurt — and
so embarrassed!

Ever since, whenever I pass by there or see
any of the girls from the old school, they all
stop and stare at me. Sometimes they laugh,
sometimes they call my name for no reason, and
sometimes they even shout something nasty.

Once I happened to be near my old school when the dismissal bell rang. Hundreds of girls with their schoolbags on their backs poured out of the building and headed home, in all different directions.

I noticed that a few girls had stopped and were whispering and looking at me. I just turned and quickly walked away. I didn't want to be the object of their secrets.

I heard them coming up behind me, so I started walking faster.

"Look, there's Blumie."

"She's not in our school anymore."

"She's running away." "Blumie...Blumie!"

I began to run. I felt like a cat being chased by some troublemaking boys.

I ran into a building I knew, and down the stairs. I found a place to hide in the basement. They followed me into the building, but started walking upstairs.

"She thinks we won't find her," someone said.

Another voice said, "Come on, let's go up to the top floor."

Then I heard Rachel's voice. "Why can't you just leave her alone?" she asked. "What did she ever do to you?" Rachel was a really good girl in the fifth grade.

Well, the girls kept running and searching, while I shrank smaller and smaller in my hiding place in the basement. I could still make out their voices, even though they were many floors above me. I just prayed that they would all leave.

Sure enough, after a while they gave up, laughing and saying that next time I wouldn't get away. Their voices faded and I...I was pressed against a door, holding onto its cold handle, when I finally broke down and cried. I stood there for a while, just sobbing quietly.

I felt so sad...and then the sadness turned into hatred. I hated those girls who had made me run away even though I hadn't done anything bad. I hated them for showing me how a chased cat feels.

Suddenly I sensed that I was not alone. From the corner of my eye I saw Rachel standing not too far from me.

As I told you, Rachel is a really good girl. Even though she's younger than me, I've always admired her.

I could see she wanted to say something, but she wasn't sure she should. She opened her mouth, and then she closed it again. Then, she put her hand on my shoulder. "Blumie," she said, "listen to me."

"WHAT?" I said angrily, and I didn't even turn around.

"Listen, I think those girls are doing something awful," she said. "If I didn't know that they were just being nasty, I would think they were really bad girls."

This sentence confused me and I turned to look at her. "I don't know what you mean," I said.

"I can tell you think those girls are running after you like that because they're bad," she said softly. "But I'm sure they're doing it without thinking at all — for no good reason, maybe because they're bored."

"Well, I don't care whether they're doing it because they're bored or because they're bad," I answered Rachel. "I'll never forgive them! You don't know what they've done to me! They've made my life miserable!"

Rachel was surprised. "What are you afraid of?" she asked me. "They're younger and smaller than you!"

I didn't have an answer for her. I just couldn't explain it. "I'm not afraid they'll hit me," I finally said. "They really hurt my feelings. You have no idea how embarrassing it is when so many girls start talking about you behind your back, and then run after you. You can't imagine how horrible I feel when they all stare at me and laugh."

Rachel nodded. "You're right," she said. "I guess that until the same thing happens to me, I won't really know what it's like. Yes, you are absolutely right," she said again.

Suddenly I felt like she had taken some of my pain for herself, and I felt better.

"Let me think about this and see if I can come up with some way to help. I'll call you," she said, and with a friendly pat on my back, she walked off.

A few days passed, and I was afraid to leave my house. I'd run home from my new school down a back street and lock my door. If my old school let out later, I'd close the curtains in my house so that I could peek out a drop but the girls couldn't see me. There were still a few of them who insisted on pointing at my house and whispering.

Then Rachel called me. She told me that she had spoken to some of her classmates and told them what the others were doing to me. "They don't all know who you are," she said, "but they came up with a great idea. Tomorrow we are all going to stand together with you near the gate to the schoolyard and show the others that we are on your side. Soon enough they'll figure out that if they want to start up with you, they'll have to take us all on!"

Baruch Hashem, it worked. The others quickly stopped their taunting for good. But now I want to tell kids everywhere: Think about the things you do. Maybe it's fun to feel big and strong and to make fun of another kid. But you should know that that kind of fun is like a knife! Your laughter can cut up a kid's feelings without you even noticing, cut him so badly that he might never heal.

The Torah teaches us that embarrassing someone is like murder! Well, that's how I felt. I'm sure that if everyone would think about it, they would realize that they really don't want to do something so bad. I mean, doesn't everybody really want to be good?

A Dangerous Game

My name is Yechezkel. I live in Beersheva, and I'm in the seventh grade.

On the very first day of school this year, our teacher told us that seventh grade was going to be different. "You are big boys now, and some of you will reach Bar Mitzvah age this year. So you might as well start acting now like adults. That means thinking carefully about everything you do."

Boy, did those words make us feel great! We would be taken seriously, and treated like men already.

But then nothing really changed from the way things had been before. It's embarrassing to admit, but we still played the same games, and we still fought over the same silly things we'd fought about before.

And then, in Shevat, one of our classmates — Yossi — surprised us with invitations to his

Bar Mitzvah celebration. It was going to be held in a small catering hall in town.

I was so excited — and proud! One of us was about to accept the "yoke of mitzvos." The invitation felt like a certificate of adulthood. I had never gotten my own personal invitation to anything before. I displayed it in a prominent place in our house so everyone in my family could see it and be impressed.

And the other kids in the class? they felt exactly the same way.

Well, the big day arrived. Naturally, we kids were the first to show up at the hall. We sat right down at our table; we sang and we felt ten feet tall.

Then the speeches started, and we got to feeling bored, so we all slipped out for some air. In the parking lot outside the hall, there was a kind of a wagon belonging to the telephone company. I don't know if "wagon" is the right word. It was some sort of contraption on wheels that telephone repairmen use for their work. On the front was a thick metal bar that worked like a brake.

Well, we started climbing on the thing, and then somebody released the bar, and we felt ourselves moving. Down the hill we went for half a minute or so, till suddenly there was a

BANG! The wagon crashed into a big garbage dumpster at the edge of the parking lot and stopped.

I know this sounds ridiculous, but we all got a kick out of it. We didn't think that this might be dangerous, and we dragged the wagon back up the hill so we could try to do it again, only better.

Now, thinking back to this dangerous game, I can't believe we were so stupid. I'm very angry at myself for not realizing that it was only a matter of time until something terrible happened. We kept repeating it — dragging the wagon up the hill and speeding down on it.

Along the way, Eli discovered a way to improve on the idea and make our ride even more exciting. He sat himself on top of the wagon, and then, midway down, he'd pull back on the bar. The wagon would abruptly stop, and all of us would go flying. Whoever managed to hang on was the "winner." For some reason, we thought this was funny. It was like one of the rides in an amusement park.

And you know something? We forgot all about the Bar Mitzvah. We forgot that we had come to celebrate with our friend. We forgot him completely.

Then things started getting really dangerous. Some of the boys were getting hurt when

they fell off. I decided to stop climbing onto the wagon. I was just plain scared. But don't think it occurred to me to tell the rest of the kids to stop. Nope. I just watched from the side and enjoyed it, and I even helped them drag the thing back up the hill each time.

Then, the accident happened right before my eyes. The wagon flew, heading at top speed for the garbage dumpster. Eli wasn't on it this time, but I saw him chasing it. It looked like he wanted to pull the brake before it slammed into the dumpster. He was racing toward the front of it.

"Watch out!" I screamed at him. "You can't!" But he didn't hear.

He threw himself at the bar, but he didn't have time to pull back on it. The wagon knocked him into the dumpster.

All of a sudden there was absolute silence. All the boys stood with their mouths open in horror.

"Move the wagon! Fast!" I screamed.

Shaking, we all pushed the wagon away. Eli slipped to the ground.

We circled him and started screaming, "Eli! Eli! Answer us." But there was no way Eli could answer us. He was blue, and you could see he wasn't breathing.

"Eli, please!"

No response.

Then — I can't explain why, exactly, and I found out later that what I did could have made things worse — I went over to him and slapped him really hard on the back. I guess I was remembering what my mother always does when one of us has something stuck in his throat.

No response. His face was turning gray. Then I hit him again, hard. I was crazy. I just kept hitting him until suddenly I heard some kind of strange sound come from his chest. He seemed to start breathing — but very weakly.

By now all the guests had come out of the hall. One of them was a doctor. He started doing mouth-to-mouth resuscitation on Eli. Someone else called an ambulance. Eli was still unconscious when they took him to the hospital.

For days, Eli was in critical condition. The whole country was saying *tehillim* for him. There was even a notice in the newspaper asking people to *daven* for Eli ben Chana.

And we boys — you can just imagine — we walked around during those days with our heads down. We couldn't look at anyone. More than anything else, we were frightened. We were scared that, God forbid, Eli wouldn't make it. And we all felt it was our fault.

I went to the hospital with my friends to visit Eli. But at the entrance to the floor, we were stopped by Eli's father. He was standing there with a doctor, and both of them were wearing white coats.

"Eli's condition is critical," he told us. I thought he'd be angry, but his face was so full of worry there wasn't room for anything else. "Please just *daven* very hard for him," Eli's father said.

They wouldn't let us into Eli's room. We peeked in, but all we could see were machines and tubes — we couldn't see Eli at all.

We prayed and we prayed and we cried so hard that we must have been heard in *shamayim.* Then, an unbelievable miracle happened — Eli's condition began to improve. He slowly and steadily got better until they said he was out of danger!

On Shabbos, I walked over to the hospital with some friends to visit Eli. He was sitting up in bed. As soon as I came into the room, he turned to his mother and said, "Imma, this is the boy who helped me start breathing again."

I was shocked. How could he have known that? Then Eli told me something amazing. When he first was crushed, he hadn't really lost consciousness yet. He had felt a terrible need to breathe, but he just couldn't do it! "Your banging

somehow got me started again," he explained.
"You saved my life!"

I hardly ever cry, and if I do, I go where no
one will see me. But at that moment, I began to
cry right in front of everybody, and they all cried
right along with me.

It was hard for me to write this story. For
a long time I couldn't even talk about it. But
I decided I had to, so that others could easily
learn what I had to learn the hard way. Please,
before you do anything, think about what it
could lead to!

If you read this story a second time, and I'm
sure you will, you will find a number of serious
mistakes that I made, along with the other boys.
That's the way it always is: "One *averah* leads
to another." It starts with a little playing around
at a Bar Mitzvah celebration, and look where it
can end.

Oh, and Yossi — the boy whose Bar Mitzvah celebration was totally ruined — just think
about him. I apologized and so did the others,
but do you think we'll ever be able to look him
in the eye again? You only become Bar Mitzvah
once in your life, and you only have one Bar
Mitzvah celebration, and we really messed his
up good!

I guess you could say that one positive thing
came out of all this — we grew up. Finally we

became more serious. Maybe it was seeing all that pain and the horrible results of our own stupidity that made the difference.

Baruch Hashem, Eli got better and came back to class. But it was a big shame that we had to grow up this way and pay such a heavy price.

My name is Gila. I am eleven, and I'm in the sixth grade. I'm quite a good student and I have little brothers. Sometimes I get so mad at them that I think I won't be able to control myself anymore, and in one more second I will explode. But now I decided that you don't always have to get angry and annoyed. So I sat down to think what I could do. How can I make this better?

So I suddenly got a great idea! Are they making you mad? Are they bothering you? Then just: PATIENCE and FORGIVENESS!

I hope you will also enjoy my idea and that you will have a lot of help from Hashem.

From Gila.

Dear Chaim Walder the Author:

Two days ago it was Friday and I came home from a school trip and I was hungry and tired. And I was thinking of not really helping my mother in the house for shabbos and just going straight to sleep but then I thought of you Chaim and all your stories, and I just decided that I would help my mother and then I started to help and help so much that I forgot I was tired at all. And I really want to thank you because even on Fridays I think about your stories.

Thank you very much,
Brocha.

My Special Brother

My name is Shira, and I'm in the fifth grade. I'm not one to tell stories about myself. I'm usually quiet and shy. But this time I'll make an exception, because it's been hard for me to keep this story to myself.

See, I'm the oldest of the kids in our family. I have five younger brothers and sisters.

After me comes a brother. Only, he's not like other kids. He was born that way. He's never said a word and he never seems to hear anything. He has some problem I can't explain exactly, but it's a serious one. The doctors call him "autistic." They say this is the name for someone who can't make any connection with people or the world around him. But we just call him Benjy — that's his name.

My parents care a lot about Benjy. They

take him to the best doctors, and they hire special teachers for him. Because my parents have worked so hard, my brother has actually made a lot of progress. The doctors are amazed that someone with such a serious problem has accomplished so much.

So, that part's good. But I have to admit that I felt a little sorry for myself for a long time. Deep inside, I felt that my parents were spending all their time on Benjy, and that they were kind of...forgetting about me. I mean, I knew that it wasn't because they loved him more than they loved me. I understood that he needed more time and attention for everything. But, even though I understood, it still bothered me.

Years passed, and I got used to the fact that everything in the house centered around Benjy. Parents never home, rest times, family trips — everything was decided by Benjy and what was good for him.

How about what was good for me? No one ever asked.

Of course, my mother always praised me a lot. "Without Shira," she told everyone, "I could never manage."

It felt good to hear that, but my heart always ached: I could use some attention too, and maybe even some concern. Why did it all have to go to my brother?

Then this year, something happened. It was during *Chol Ha-Mo'ed Sukkos*. My parents had promised us a trip up north. The day came, but my parents decided my brother was in no shape to come with us.

At first, my father thought he'd put the trip off for another time. But the little kids started to cry. What should they do? My father would have to go, because he's the driver. So my mother said she'd stay home.

But my brothers and sisters refused to go on a trip without Imma. And I could tell by my father's eyes that he also would be sad if he had to spend the day driving the kids around without Imma.

"I'll stay," I heard myself say.

My mother was surprised. "You, Shira? With Benjy?"

"Sure," I said with confidence. "Don't you trust me?"

"No, Shira, I don't want you to say home," my mother protested. "I want you to go and have a good time."

Well, we talked about it for a while, and finally my parents both agreed to go. Boy, did I feel good — so grown-up!

They left and the house got very quiet. Benjy was on the floor, making the little noises that he always makes to himself.

I looked at him. He just kept staring at a picture on the wall, and didn't seem to even know that I was there with him.

I realized that I had never been alone with my brother before. I had never really tried to make contact with him.

Oh, well. I started playing with some Lego. I got very interested in what I was building and I forgot about my brother. First I made a house with a couple of windows and a red chimney. After that I made a car, and then I attached its wheels and stuck in a driver.

Suddenly I remembered Benjy. He was looking at the car I had made. I even thought I saw a tiny bit of interest in his eyes.

"Do you want the car?" I asked him.

He didn't answer. He just kept staring at it.

I went over to him, and opened up his hands. I put the car into them. He held it for a minute, then he just pulled his hands away, letting the car fall onto the floor and break.

"Benjy!" I screamed. "Why? Why did you break my car?"

He just looked down at the smashed car with his usual empty stare. It was like he had never seen it before. He didn't care about it in the least — not like me who had just spent the last twenty-five minutes working on it.

It was too much, even for a quiet girl like me.

"Why do you always have to ruin everything for me?" I screamed at him.

He was still looking at the broken car.

"Answer me, do you hear? ANSWER ME!"

I put my hands on either side of his head, and I turned it so that he was facing me. Then I said, "This time I'm not going to let you get away with it. Look me in the eye and tell me: Why did you do it?"

He didn't seem to mind my holding him so hard. But he had that empty look about him. We stayed close like that for a few moments. His head was in my hands, and we were face to face.

Then I thought I saw a teardrop in his eye. I relaxed my hold and his head came to rest on my shoulder. I felt him almost cuddle against me, and his hands held onto me.

Suddenly I understood. I realized that my parents gave Benjy so much attention because he would never feel anything if they treated him like the rest of us. I realized that just like my mother says "I love you" to me and I understand her, she wants him to understand too. And, in order to get him to understand — even just a little — he has to be told in a very special way, a way that usually takes a lot of time and a lot of effort.

Benjy picked up his head and looked at me. His eyes were not as glazed as before, and I thought that this time he really might be seeing me.

"I love you," I said to Benjy for the first time in my life. And he must have understood, because he hugged me.

The Boom Boom Man

My name is Ariel. I'm in the sixth grade and I think my story is important for all of you to know.

One day our teacher gave us a lot of homework. I decided I would just stay at my desk after school until I finished it. I called home and told my mother I'd be late.

Then I was all alone in the classroom. What a strange feeling. The entire school building was quiet. Suddenly, from the first floor, I heard some banging. BOOM, BOOM, BOOM. I didn't really think about it very much at first. The banging kept on at a steady rate, and after a little while I got used to it. Then it stopped. But a minute or so later, the banging started up again. This time the noise was louder and it sounded closer to me. BOOM! BOOM!

I'm not a scaredy-cat, believe me. But now fear started creeping into my whole body.

I stopped doing my homework and just listened. I realized what I was hearing followed a kind of pattern. There were thirty booms and then a minute of quiet. Then the noise would start up somewhere else.

Suddenly, I heard steps on the staircase. Someone was coming nearer! Why was I here? Why didn't I think before I decided to stay late? I held my breath and then the booms started again. This time they were coming from the classroom right next door. I started shaking and couldn't stop.

Then sure enough, the steps started coming in my direction... I was so scared! At the last minute, I jumped up and hid under my chair. The door opened... I peeked out through the desk legs and I saw a pair of dirty boots standing in the doorway. And then a voice said, "Boy, am I mad. I'm really burning mad!" And the boots walked into the room.

I carefully peeked up to see the face that belonged with that voice and those boots. I saw an older man, very tall and with a big moustache. He had a scary face — well, hadn't he just said he was mad?

Then came a very loud boom. Of course! Now I could see he was just picking up our classroom chairs and putting them on our desks.

I shrank down into my hiding place. But it

was hopeless. Soon he would find me.

The man got to my row. He picked up the chairs at the first desk, then the second, and then there he was standing over me. He looked like a giant!

He was shocked to see me. "Who are you?" asked the man. "What are you doing here at this hour?"

I didn't answer. I was still shaking.

"And besides," thundered the man, "why don't you ever pick up your chair?"

I started to cry!

"Oh, stop," said the man, "I didn't mean any-thing. I was just talking." But I couldn't calm down.

"That's enough crying now. If you don't stop, I'll start crying right along with you," said the man, and he looked so sorry that I managed to stop.

He looked relieved, and then he laughed a tired laugh. "I'll even give you a candy," he said. "Just please forgive me for making you cry." He began looking through all his pockets, but in the end all he found was an old candy wrapper. "This is all I have for now," he said with a shrug. "You'll get the candy another time."

I laughed. I had to admit this was not a very scary person after all. He sure acted a lot nicer than he looked.

"Why are you so upset?" I asked him, still on my guard.

"Listen," he said, sitting down on the nearest desk — which looked like a little stool under him. "My job in this school is to sweep and wash the floors. I've been doing it for twenty years.

"When I first started, that was all I had to do — sweep and wash. There were never any chairs on the floor when I started to work here. I don't know when things started to change. It wasn't all at once. At first, one or two kids would forget to pick up their chairs. So, no problem. I would just pick up that chair or two without thinking anything of it. Then it would be a few kids in every class. But for the past few years, nobody in the whole school has remembered to pick up his chair. I have to do all of them by myself!"

I was amazed. No one had ever told us to pick up our chairs.

"Think a minute," he said. "If every boy picked up his chair, it wouldn't be a very big deal for him. But for me, at my age, to pick up 550 chairs every day...do you know how hard that is for me?"

I couldn't speak. This new idea filled my whole head. Here was something right in front of my eyes that I had never thought of before this very minute! It was frightening. Day after day, without one second's thought, my friends and I had run out of the classroom and left this poor man with a lot of work that he shouldn't have had to do. We had made his job twice as hard. How much pain we had caused him!

"Let me help you," was all I could think of to say, and I began to pick up all the rest of the chairs in the room. Then I ran upstairs to the third floor and put all the chairs there on the desks.

Let me tell you, it wasn't easy. I thought, if only the kids knew how hard this was, each one would do his share.

I suddenly remembered to look at my watch. It was getting late. "My mother won't know what happened to me," I called to the janitor, as I grabbed my book bag and ran out the door.

That night, I had trouble falling asleep. I kept thinking about the man I had met, the school janitor, whose name I didn't even know. And I kept thinking about how it must happen all the time that we do things without thinking that cause problems for other people. Finally, I decided there was something I could do about this one, at least. I'm pretty shy, but I decided I would do it anyway. And once I made the decision, I fell asleep.

The next morning, I got to school early, and as soon as the teacher came in, I went over to him and told him what had happened. He was amazed. "Why didn't he ever speak up?" he said, shaking his head.

I asked for permission to go around to all the classes and explain why everyone should pick up his chair and put it on his desk before going home each day. The teacher smiled and told me to go. He even made a suggestion. He said he would choose two monitors and put them in charge of this job. They would stay after school to make sure everyone remembered to do it, write down the name of anyone who forgot, and pick up his chair for him.

Right after *davening*, I started on the first floor and went from class to class telling the story that I told you about the janitor. I could see that it made an impression on all the kids. I also told them about the idea that my teacher had for monitors. It took me an hour to cover all the classrooms. In the end, I felt really good.

About two weeks later, as I was leaving school, I saw a familiar face waiting for me at the gate. It was the janitor.

As soon as he spotted me, he gave me a big smile. Then he took me in his gigantic hands, and lifted me up in the air.

Putting me down, he said, "You! I don't know how you did it, but I'm sure it was you. You have no idea how much easier you have made my life." Then he said, "You know, I don't even know your name."

"Ariel," I answered him. "What's yours?"

"My name is Yosef," he replied. I could tell he wanted to say something more to thank me, but he couldn't find the words. So he just said, "You should always be well! You will get your reward from Heaven for this wonderful thing you did for me."

I waved goodbye and walked off. Then I heard a voice calling, "Ariel, Ariel!" I turned around and I saw that he was coming after me. "I forgot," he said. He started searching through his pockets and then he took out a candy. "This is nothing," he said. "It's just something I owe you. Remember?"

I put it in my pocket and I thought, I won't eat it. I'll save it to remember this whole story forever. Because, the truth is that thinking about the good thing I had done was a lot sweeter than any candy.

Oh — and it didn't have a wrapper. The candy, that is.

There's Hope!

My name is Avi and my problem is that I am just too STRONG! Everybody's afraid of me...because I hit other kids. All the grown-ups ask me why I hit, but I don't answer them because they don't understand me, and anyway, I myself don't know.

I mean, yesterday I hit Moshe, a kid in my class. Moshe used to be a lazy little kid. Then, all of a sudden, he got to be this really serious student. He got so good that our teacher's always praising him. He did it so much one day, that I felt really jealous. So, during recess, I just went over and hit him. The teacher punished me, Moshe's mad at me, and the rest of the kids — they hate me anyway.

I'm also a rotten student. I don't understand anything the teacher says. I try to — I do — but I still don't know what's going on. The teacher insists I'm not trying, but that's not true! I just

CAN'T. If only I could be like Ephraim.

Ephraim understands everything. He is the smartest kid in the whole class. He always knows the answers when I don't even under-stand the questions. Ephraim is a quiet boy — he never brags or makes a big show. I really like him, but he never pays any attention to me. Boy, would I like to sit next to him and be as smart as he is and have the whole class like me the way they like him. But nobody cares about me. They all think I just want to be bad. They think I LIKE to beat up kids.

I'm telling you, it's not true. I want to be everybody's friend, and I want all of them to want to be my friends. But it won't happen, because they're all afraid of me.

If only somebody could explain to them that I am just a regular kid like they are. All I want is a chance. Just one tiny chance — for someone to play with me or come to my house. I wish once the teacher would say something nice about me…my parents, too.

But nobody plays with me because they're afraid I'll hit them. And the teacher doesn't have anything good to say about me, because I'm always doing bad things. And what would my parents praise me for? I just make trouble for them.

I look really strong on the outside. But you

know what? I'm just an unhappy kid. Sometimes at night, when nobody hears, I cry. In the daytime, I would never let anyone see me cry. And to make sure they don't think I'm a crybaby, I hit them! But just you and I know the truth.

I've thought many times of going around to all the kids I ever hit and apologizing to them — telling them it'll never happen again. But, you know, I'm afraid. I'm afraid they'll just laugh at me.

Yesterday, the teacher spoke to us about *teshuvah.* He said that every Jew, even if he did bad things all year long, has a chance in the month of Elul to ask Hashem and the people he hurt to forgive him. The teacher said that Hashem only forgives us for the things we did to other people if we ask those people to forgive us.

Then the teacher suggested that we ask everyone in the class to forgive us. And he reminded us that if someone doesn't forgive his friend, Hashem won't forgive *him!*

I decided this was my chance. If I didn't do it now, I never would. So I found my courage, and I walked over to one kid that I had smacked during the year, and I told him I was sorry. You won't believe it — he said he forgave me! Then I went to a few others, and they all forgave me!

One even said, "Hey, you know, I always wanted to be your friend, but I didn't think you wanted to be mine."

Going around like that and saying I was sorry was really, really hard. But now that I got started, I feel good. Tomorrow I'm going to speak to the rest of the kids in my class and tell them that I'm sorry.

Elul is a great time to do *teshuvah*. I don't want to let it get by me this year. Do you think there's hope for me?

My name : Esther

I am nine and a half, and my father is not religious but my mother believes in Hashem. My father tells me to switch over to a school that isn't religious but I don't want to. My father says I have to. He doesn't want me to wash before I eat bread and he wants me to do a lot of things that people who aren't religious do. I don't want to do not religious things, and he doesn't let... I hope I can still stay strong and maybe my father will let me stay in my school.

My name is Mordechai and I live in Bnei Brak.

Last year, when I was in fifth grade, something very upsetting happened to me. It was two days before Lag Ba-Omer and I wanted to ride my bicycle. I went downstairs to unchain it and suddenly my heart sank. The front wheel was missing.

When I had passed in the morning on my way to school, the bicycle had been in its place, fine and whole. And now how would I ride a one-wheeled bicycle?

I decided to go around to the neighbors to ask if they had seen or heard anything about the bicycle. But everyone answered in the negative. Only one boy, seven years old, said that he had seen a man coming out of the hallway with a wheel in his hand, turning towards Rabbi Akiva street. But in my opinion, the boy made that story up.

I tried to find the missing wheel but I have not found it.

Until this very day, I cannot understand how the borrower could have borrowed the wheel from my bicycle without permission and still not bother to return it to me.

Freddy

My name is Ilana. I'm eleven and I'm in the fifth grade. I do okay in school, except that I don't have any friends.

I'll tell you why. I'm afraid. I'm afraid that if I make a good friend and I lose her, I'll never get over it, the same way I never got over losing Freddy.

I lost Freddy four years ago, when I was seven. And I still miss him so much.

He was a giant, huggable teddy bear. My father bought him for me the day I was born. He said that when they told him in the hospital that he had a new daughter, he wanted to buy something wonderful for her, and he couldn't decide what it should be. So he went into a toy store and picked out the biggest thing they had! And that just happened to be Freddy, my teddy bear.

My father likes telling me how the nurses

in the hospital laughed at him for buying such a huge "thing" — that's what they called it — for such a tiny baby. But I loved this present more than anything. When I got a little bigger, I started to call him Freddy, and I took the best care of him. I used to dust him off and sit him down in the corner of my room. I loved to put necklaces around his neck. I enjoyed his just *being* there.

When I began first grade, my parents started hinting to me that it was time to get rid of Freddy. "You're a big girl now," they said, "and a teddy bear like that is not for you anymore."

But I was very attached to my Freddy, and so my parents stopped talking about it. "It'll pass," I once heard my mother say quietly to my father.

But it didn't pass. I couldn't let go of Freddy, even though I could see he looked a little ridiculous to people. I just felt very close to him. I guess I'm the kind of girl who has trouble saying goodbye — even if it's just to an ordinary teddy bear. But, let me tell you, Freddy is no ordinary teddy bear.

By the time I was in second grade and still very attached to Freddy, my parents got worried. He was looking awfully old and shabby, and they really thought I was too big... But they still didn't insist that I throw him away — they only hinted at it once in a while.

One day, I came home from school, and when I went into my room, I screamed, "Where's Freddy?"

My parents both ran in. "What happened?" they asked.

I pointed to the corner where Freddy always sat. "He's gone!"

We all began to search the house. But Freddy wasn't so little, and it didn't take us long to realize that he wasn't anywhere in the house.

Then my mother remembered. "There was a new cleaning lady here today. Maybe she threw him out?"

We called up the cleaning lady, who couldn't seem to understand exactly who Freddy was. But I explained. Then she said, "Oh, you mean that big doll on the floor that looked like an old rag? I tried to throw it out with the trash, but just then somebody passed by and asked if he could have the thing, so I gave it to him."

A rag. She called my Freddy a rag. And she gave him to a stranger.

That day I couldn't speak. I just couldn't say a word. And the next day, too. On the third day, my mother sat down next to me and said, "Ilana, that's enough. You cannot mope so long over a worn out doll. Stop."

I began to cry. I cried for an hour, maybe, until I had no strength left in me.

Three years have passed since then, but I still miss my Freddy. Sometimes I dream about him. I usually dream that something bad happened to him; I never dream that he is happy. I miss him and I think about him all the time.

And along the way, I finished second grade. And then third grade and fourth grade. Now I'm in fifth.

I know I'm big already, but I still miss that bear. And because of it, I never got too friendly with anyone. I figure that if I ever made a close friend and then lost her — maybe she'd get tired of me or just decide to be someone else's friend instead — I'd never be able to stand the pain.

Anyway, last week I got a call from a neighbor across the street, Mrs. Chasson. She asked if I could come over that evening to babysit.

I never babysat before, and I was really excited. Somebody finally thought I was big enough to take care of their kids.

At seven o'clock, I went over to the Chasson house. It was a small house, not very fancy. I'd heard that the Chassons didn't have much money.

Mrs. Chasson introduced me to her children, and she told me all the things I had to do.

At first, I played with them in the living room for a while. Then, at eight o'clock, I announced, "Everybody to bed!"

They all went nicely. I tucked Yochanan, who was four, into bed and covered him. And then I put the baby Meira to sleep. When that was done, I said to Zehavah, who was seven, "You're the oldest. I bet you can get into bed by yourself."

"Of course I can," she said. She walked over to her bed, and lifted the cover...

There, just as cute as ever, was Freddy, my teddy bear. I was shocked. I looked at him and tears came to my eyes.

"What's the matter?" asked Zehavah, alarmed.

I tried to smile, and I asked, "What's that?"

"That's my teddy bear, can't you see?" answered Zehavah. "Abba gave him to me a long, long time ago, and I keep him in my bed. But, why are you crying?" she asked me.

I picked him up. Yes, this was my Freddy. No question about it. I touched the place where his eye had been, before it fell out, while he was still mine.

"I love him even though he has a missing eye. My parents laugh at me, but I don't care," said Zehavah.

I held Freddy a moment longer, trying to think if there was anything I could do. But of course, I knew there was no way I could break Zehavah's heart. And, anyway, an eleven-year-old babysitter with a teddy bear? It was really kind of silly, I guess.

Then, all of a sudden, I felt the pain I had been storing up since the second grade leave my heart. All those years of sadness over losing Freddy disappeared right there on the spot. I had been worried that maybe he was being mistreated. But now I saw that someone loved him very much.

"You're taking good care of him, right?" I asked.

"Of course! Forever and ever."

"And you'll be careful not to let the cleaning lady give him away to someone else?" I asked.

"Cleaning lady? What cleaning lady?" asked the little girl. "We don't have money for a cleaning lady to come to our house. My mother sometimes cleans other people's houses. And my mother knows how much I love my teddy bear."

"Just be careful," I said to her, "that you don't lose him."

"Lose him? My teddy bear? Never. When I get bigger, I'm going to give him to my baby sister, and I'll make sure she takes good care of him, just like I do."

I felt a special kind of happiness fill my heart. At last there was an end to my story, a happy ending — someone would always love and take care of my Freddy.

"So what's his name?" I asked.

Zehavah thought for a second. "He doesn't have a name," she said. "He's just a teddy bear."

"Well, I think he has a name," I said. "His name is Freddy."

Zehavah looked at me as if I just came from outer space. "WHAT?"

"That's what his name is," I said. "Don't you like it?"

Zehavah thought for a minute. Then she said, "You know, I think it's a good name. I'll call him Freddy from now on."

The Pressure Cooker

My name is Menasheh. I'm eleven, and I'm a real quiet kid. I'd like to tell you my story, and then I'd like to make a very important request.

First, the story. It happened about a month ago. I came home from school with my brother Yonasan. The door was locked, so we got the key from our neighbor and opened it.

There was a note for us on the kitchen table. My mother had written that she had to go out for something, and she had left our snack in the refrigerator. At the end, my mother wrote, "Do not touch the pot on the stove."

The first thing I did was look toward the stove. Sure enough, the pressure cooker was on one of the burners. The fire was off, but you could see the pot was still hot. Do you know what a pressure cooker is? It's a heavy steel pot, with the top screwed on tight. You can cook things in it without their boiling over.

The pot has two openings with stoppers on them. You can open them carefully to let out steam. Without the holes to let the steam out, the pot would just explode from all the pressure inside.

I don't know what came over me. I always listen to my parents. But this time, my curiosity got the better of me, and I decided to play around with the pot as soon as my brother left the kitchen.

So, the first thing I did was pull out the stoppers. Right away, a thin stream of steam shot out. I thought that was kind of neat. So I decided to open up the pot, and see how the openings looked from the inside.

Well, anyone who knows anything about a pressure cooker is probably frightened about what I'll say next. Because it is absolutely forbidden to open a pressure cooker while it is hot. ABSOLUTELY. But I didn't know that. Not then.

It took a lot of effort, but I finally got the pot half-way open. Suddenly, a powerful spray of steam covered my hand.

The pain! I think the pain that I felt at that moment was the worst that anybody could ever feel. My hand felt on fire, dried up and burning. Oh, how it burned!

First, I thought about my mother: Boy is she going to give it to me! Then I thought: HELP! My hand is really burning!

I could barely think straight. But somehow I ran over to where my mother keeps her giant, metal mixing bowl and filled it with cold tap water. I put it on the table and started dunking my hand into it. I kept my hand under water until the water turned warm. As soon as I pulled my hand out of the water, I felt the awful pain. I had to plunge my hand back into the water to keep from screaming.

I was beginning to panic. I knew that I had done something really terrible to my hand, but I was more worried about what my mother would do to me when she found out. I didn't want her to know — ever!

I must have refilled the bowl with cold water at least ten times before Yonasan came back into the kitchen. "What are you doing?" I heard him asking, even though my mind was elsewhere. "Don't you have anything better to do?"

"Just don't tell Imma," I begged.

Then he saw my hand. He looked so shocked and scared that I knew I was in big trouble. "Menasheh," he said, putting his hand on my shoulder, "your hand is so red and burned! We have to call someone."

"No, no!" I screamed. And then I started to cry, "Please don't tell. I'm afraid Imma will punish me for opening the pot."

Yonasan just watched me, feeling sorry for me and afraid. He filled another bowl for me, so it was ready when the first one got warm. "Go ahead, dunk," he said. And I did, while I cried.

Yonasan said, "Menasheh, it's really bad. We *have* to call somebody for help."

"No," I begged, "please don't tell." Then I started sobbing, and I couldn't stop.

Somewhere along the line, Yonasan disappeared. Then, he came back into the kitchen with our neighbor, Mrs. Katz. He's told her, I thought.

"It's not my fault," I said to her, even though I knew it was no use, because anyone could tell it was my fault.

Mrs. Katz took one look at my hand and cried out, "*Oy vey! Oy vey!*" I guess it really was a sight. Then she got herself under control, picked up the phone, and called for an ambulance.

The ambulance came really fast, and I got in holding onto my bowl of water.

Half an hour later, my mother came to the hospital. The minute she saw me, she burst into tears and started to hug and kiss me. I was waiting for her to yell at me, but all she seemed to care about was my hand.

Well, I'll make it brief. The doctors put some special cream on my hand, and wrapped it in gauze. For a whole month, I had to put on the cream and rewrap my hand to keep it from getting infected. It hurt plenty, and it took a long time to heal. But it got better, *baruch Hashem.*

My mother told me that I'll have the scar on my hand my whole life, just like the story about Leah in *Kids Speak I.* She said I was very smart to put it in cold water as soon as it happened.

"*Baruch Hashem* you knew what to do. But I don't understand why you didn't send Yonasan to Mrs. Katz right away," my mother said.

I answered, "I thought about it, but I was afraid."

"What were you afraid of?" she asked.

"Of you," I said.

That shook her up.

"I was afraid you would punish me for touching the pressure cooker after you clearly warned us not to," I whispered, with my head down.

"Menasheh," she said with a sigh, "let me try to explain something to you. If I had seen you touching the pot, I probably would have punished you. The punishment would have been something to remind you not to try a dangerous thing like that again. But once you've learned that lesson in such a hard way, why would I need to punish you? All a mother wants is what is good for her child. Parents want their children to be safe, and not to get hurt.

"I hope nothing bad will ever happen to

you again," added my mother. "But I beg you, Menasheh, don't keep things from me because you're afraid of what I'll say. No one loves you more than your father and I do. You had to suffer a lot because you didn't understand that."

Anyway, I'm going to tell you what my mother asked of me: If, God forbid, something bad ever happens to you — whether it's something you did to yourself or something someone else did to you — don't be afraid to tell your parents. I promise you, they won't punish you — they'll just want to help you.

I didn't do that... I'm just lucky that I had a brother smart enough to tell on me.

You're Right!

My name is Baily and I'm in the fourth grade. I'm a good student, and I get along with all the girls in the class. All of them.

I never had a fight with anyone, and no one has ever done anything bad to me or spoken against me or anything like that. You must have someone like me in your class, and you probably think it's no problem for him or her to get along with the whole world. Well, it's not that simple.

There are twenty-five girls in my class, and each one is different from the others. There are tall ones and short ones, smart ones and not so smart ones, strong ones and weak ones, brave ones and scaredy-cats. Everyone has good points and bad points, including me.

Fights start when one girl doesn't understand the other one, or maybe disagrees with something she's said. Sometimes I see kids fighting for the dumbest reasons! And that's a problem for me, because I want to go over and tell them so. But I have a rule: NEVER get involved in a fight that has nothing to do with me. Because it can only get me in trouble, and it won't help the other kids either.

Sure, sometimes other girls can make me angry. And then I have to use all my strength to control myself. It used to be very hard for me. I would really boil inside, even if I didn't show it on the outside. But after I got used to keeping my mouth shut, I started being able to laugh at a lot of the things that kids fight about.

Sometimes a girl will say, "She looked at me!" and start a fight about it! Or one will make a big deal over the kid behind her kicking her chair. Or someone will yell if someone else gets ahead of her in line to wash for lunch.

These things used to bother me, but I learned to see them differently. Like, what's the big deal if somebody looks at me? (I mean, wouldn't it be really sad if no one looked at me?) And if someone behind me kicks my chair, I just have to ask her nicely to stop it. And, when we're standing in line to wash, why should I fight? So what if I start eating my sandwich half a minute later? And, if I fight over *netilas yadayim*, I make it into a mitzvah that came through an *averah*.

There are loads and loads of examples of fights that would never happen if only kids would think for one second before starting them. So that's what I do: I stop to think for a second before I get angry. And I always calm down.

Sometimes two girls come over to me — each one with her side of the story why the other is wrong, and each one asking me to take her side.

That's the worst! Because, besides their own fight, I'll also end up in a fight with one of them. And that's no good.

That's why I never take sides. Never ever. And there's something I sometimes do that I once heard in a story. (Maybe you've heard it too?) I listen carefully to each of them, and then say they are both right.

In fact, the whole thing actually happened to me once — just like in the story. Malky and Gittie were having an argument, and they came to me to complain about each other.

First, Malky started telling me why she was angry at Gittie. I listened, and I said to her, "You're right." Then Gittie told me why she was angry at Malky. And I told her, "You're right." Meanwhile, Rena had been standing nearby listening, and she said: "How can it be that Malky and Gittie are both right?"

I thought about it for a minute, and then I said, "You know, you're right, too!"

It Must Be Angels

My name is Ezra. I live in Netanya, and I'm in the seventh grade. My best friend Uzi is also in my class. He happens to be exactly two days older than me. He also lives on my block so we always walk to school and back home together.

One day, we were walking home like we usually do when we saw, down at the end of the street, funny old Mr. Baum. He was trying to nail two boards together.

Uzi asked him, "What are you doing, Mr. Baum?"

"How about moving away?" answered the old man, annoyed. "You're blocking my light."

"Sorry," we both said, and we moved over. But Uzi was curious. "What are you building, Mr. Baum?" he asked.

Mr. Baum finally picked up his eyes from the wood and looked in our direction. "I'm building a shul," he threw the words at us. "Now get lost."

We laughed and walked away. It really tickled us to think that old Mr. Baum believed he could make a shul out of those two boards!

The next day we saw Mr. Baum banging nails again. Only this time, yesterday's two boards were connected and they were holding a third.

"What are you doing, Mr. Baum?" asked Uzi.

Mr. Baum didn't even bother to look up. "I'm building a shul, I told you," he answered.

We walked away, and suddenly a thought hit me. "I know what he's making — a *shtender*!" I said.

We began to follow the progress of this shul by walking past Mr. Baum at his work every day. We watched him build the chairs, the *bimah*, and the *aron kodesh*. He really has golden hands, that Mr. Baum.

"Where is this shul going to be?" asked Uzi one day.

"Right here," Mr. Baum was lost in his work, and just pointed with his chin in the direction of the nearby building, "on the first floor of my house."

Mr. Baum owned an old house with two floors. He always used to rent out the bottom floor to different tenants. Now he must have decided to turn it into a shul.

Months passed, and Mr. Baum was still busy building, painting, whitewashing — before our

very eyes a new shul was taking shape!

One day, we saw Mr. Baum standing on a ladder and painting a sign on the wall of his house. Soon we could make out the words: BEIS KNESSES CHASDEI EFRAYIM.

The following day there were notices posted all over town. They invited one and all to come and *daven* in the new shul called Chasdei Efrayim.

Uzi and I decided to go there at the time posted for *Minchah*. There were three people waiting there, and one of them was Mr. Baum.

Mr. Baum was happy to see us for a change. "How nice of you to come!" he said, and then he introduced us to the others. "These are my dear boys — they always came to help me." Surprised, we didn't say a word.

A few moments later, Uzi whispered to me, "Look, he doesn't have a *minyan*." But Mr. Baum was looking happy and pleased with himself.

He checked his watch and shrugged. "Oh, everyone's probably late because they're not used to the new shul yet."

Minutes passed. Three more people walked in, but they were still short four men.

Mr. Baum counted all the people and announced that he would run out to round up a *minyan*. He went outside, and soon he came back with two men who had already *daven*ed,

but who agreed to come and complete the
minyan. "We have a *minyan!*" cried Mr. Baum
happily.

"But, Mr. Baum," said Uzi, "there are only
eight men here. You need ten."

Mr. Baum looked really confused. He
started counting the men again. "*Hoshi'ah, es,
amecha,*" then he turned to me, "*ad,*" and to
Uzi, "*olam.*"*

"Oh, no, Mr. Baum, I'm sorry we didn't tell
you before," I said, "but we're only twelve. We're
not Bar Mitzvah yet."

Mr. Baum got angry at us. "So what on earth
have you been hanging around here for all these
months? Just to bother me?" In a rage, he flew
out again to round up two more men.

Eventually, at the last possible minute, they
did manage to *daven Minchah.* At that point,
Mr. Baum was beaming with joy. We stayed
there to *daven* with the rest, even though by
then Uzi was kind of insulted by all that Mr.
Baum had said. But I tried to calm him down
and I explained that the poor man was nervous
because of all his work on the shul, and trying
to get it going and everything.

Days passed, and each day Mr. Baum would
add some new piece of furniture or decoration to

* It is customary, when counting men for a *minyan,* to do so by
using the ten-word *pasuk* from *Tehillim* 28:9.

his shul. But, no matter how many seats there were, the number of *davener*s did not increase.

Every day at *Minchah* time, you could see Mr. Baum running around to people's homes, begging them to come to his shul. In fact, when he heard that some kid reached Bar Mitzvah, he would send him a special invitation, hoping that would get him to come to the *minyan*. And it would work for a week or two, and then the young men would go back to the shul they had gone to before. Mr. Baum's shul wasn't easy to get to during the day. People were used to going to the big shul in the center of town, where there were *minyanim* one after another and it was convenient for everyone.

Uzi and I kept going to Mr. Baum's shul, even though I think it just annoyed him. It's not that he really didn't like us or anything. It just made him sad that we couldn't be counted for the *minyan* and our being there kept confusing his count.

After a few weeks of seeing how miserable poor Mr. Baum was, I had an idea. "Uzi," I said to my friend, "let's go over to Shoshanim Street and try to get Mr. Baum his *minyan* from there."

Shoshanim Street is at the other end of our block, and it's a very busy street with lots of people. So we ran over there. I was too shy to speak to strangers. But Uzi wasn't. He just walked over to the first man he saw. He wasn't even wearing a *kippah*.

"*Minyan?*" Uzi asked.

"Huh?" the man responded. Then he shrugged and walked away.

Uzi went right ahead. "Sir," he said to the next man he came to, also without a *kippah*, "could you come and join us for *Minchah?*"

The man looked a little bewildered, but then he said, "I don't mind."

"Just walk down this street," Uzi pointed. "The shul is at number 33, on the first floor."

The man walked down the block as he was told, but we stayed on Shoshanim Street, looking for three more men. It took us five minutes more to find them, but we did it. They all walked right over to the new shul, and we felt really good, but...

"Uzi," I said, "let's go to the old shul, not to Mr. Baum's."

"But why?" asked Uzi.

"I don't know, I'm just afraid Mr. Baum will be angry with us again. He may not think it's such a great idea bringing in strangers off the street."

And from that day on, that's how it was. We always found some people from the street to join Mr. Baum's *Minchah*, but then we two always walked to the old shul to *daven*.

Half a year passed, and then both of us reached the age of thirteen. We each had our *aliyos* in the shul near our house where our fathers *davened*. A few days later, Uzi said, "Hey, let's go to *Chasdei Efrayim* for *Minchah*. Now we can finally be part of the *minyan*, even though I heard that Mr. Baum gets a *minyan* these days even without the people we send him from the street."

So, tall and proud, we marched right over to Mr. Baum's shul — where we hadn't been in six months.

Mr. Baum came to welcome us! "It's you," he said, almost fondly. "I can hardly recognize you. Why did you stop coming here for *Minchah*? Probably because you saw there was no *minyan*. But you should know that the only reason there was no *minyan* then was that the shul was still new and nobody knew about it. Why, since about the time you stopped coming, there's been a *minyan* every day. Even strangers right off the street, some of them not even *frum*, have been coming here to *daven*!" Mr. Baum told us proudly.

"Really?" we said together.

"Yes indeed," Mr. Baum continued. "Every day new people would walk in here. And when I asked them how they found us, they said that two boys out on the main street had asked them to come. But I don't believe that story," Mr. Baum lowered his voice and whispered to us, "because why would two boys I don't even know want to send people here from the street? What I think happened is that Hashem saw all the hard work and effort I put into building this shul, and sent two angels down to help me when He saw how disappointed I was that I couldn't get a *minyan*.

"But don't mention what I told you about the angels to anyone," he whispered in our ears, "because people won't believe it. They'll just think I'm nuts."

"You know something, Mr. Baum," I said, "you're something of an angel yourself."

Mr. Baum silently looked at us for a minute. Then, all of a sudden a light went on in his eyes. He seemed to have realized something... but he didn't say another word. He just gave each of us a warm hug.

"*Ashrei yoshvei vesecha...*," began the *chazan*.

The Hill Battle

My name is Moishy. I'm nine and I live in a pretty neighborhood in Yerushalayim.

My story is about this little hill that's near my house. It's an ordinary little hill, with some grass — not much — and some bushes, a few funny plants, anthills, and loads of rocks.

This hill was the place we kids in the neighborhood always played — from the time we were very little. We never got tired of playing there. It was a perfect place for us.

One day we were playing ball on the hill, when Nachum came along. He's our neighbor, who's eight. He had a friend with him, some kid I didn't know. Anyway, he started playing ball with his friend, and we kept on playing our game.

All of a sudden, Hillel said, real loud and mean, "Hey, Nachum! Get lost!"

"Why?" asked Nachum.

"'Cause we got here first," said Hillel.

Nachum was stunned. "What does that mean? Is this hill only yours? We always play here together."

"Are you leaving or not?" Hillel insisted.

"Why should I?" Nachum answered. "This hill is as much mine as it is yours!"

I was kind of surprised by Hillel's behavior. Why was he trying to chase another kid off the hill? I mean, from the time we were in kindergarten, we all played right here. It was the only safe place in the neighborhood where kids were free to run around. The rest was streets or playgrounds for toddlers.

Meanwhile, Shimmy and Dovid joined Hillel's side and threatened Nachum.

"I'm not going anywhere," repeated Nachum, and he just kept playing with his friend.

The ball went back and forth a few times, and then Hillel grabbed it and threw it really hard. The ball rolled all the way down the hill, and flew into the street. Just then, a huge truck passed and rolled right over his ball. It burst and flattened into a sorry-looking pancake.

We were shocked. Nachum looked at what was left of his brand new ball, and started to cry. But Hillel — and believe me, you could see even *he* was frightened by what he had done — just said, "You deserved it! I warned you, but you just wouldn't listen."

Nachum pulled his friend's arm. "Come with me," he said, and they ran down the hill together. Nachum picked up the squashed remains of his ball and off they went.

Hillel must have felt a little uncomfortable, and he said too loudly, "Now they learned their lesson. They won't bother us anymore."

I didn't agree with him so much, but the other three seemed to, so I just kept quiet.

Well, it turned out that Hillel was wrong if he thought he taught anybody a lesson. Within a few minutes, Nachum was back. And he wasn't alone. He had five friends his age with him, and they looked very threatening as they climbed up the hill.

Shimmy said, "Look what's coming."

"Who cares? Who's afraid of them anyhow?" said Hillel, and he just kept on playing.

Nachum and his friends had reached the top of the hill by now, and they were coming closer. Now I spoke, "We told you to get lost, didn't we?"

The answer came from a kid called Akiva, one of Nachum's friends, who was younger than us, but very tough-looking. "Now you guys are gonna leave," he said.

"Oh sure," we all smirked.

Suddenly Akiva lunged at us and grabbed away our ball. He spun and threw it into the middle of the street. The battle was on.

It's hard to explain what happened next. We ran after each other, beat each other up, screamed and yelled and — you won't believe it — someone even threw a rock.

We fought for a long time. The battle finally stopped when Shimmy's brother, Mutty, who's six years old, ran away from a kid who was chasing him...straight into the middle of the street! There was a terrible screeching of brakes, and a pale, frightened driver got out of his car. He breathed a sigh of relief when he saw he hadn't hit Mutty. But then, he turned to us and started screaming, "Aren't you ashamed of yourselves? This is how you behave? A child was almost killed just now because of you!"

We all ran home in different directions. It was getting dark already. When I got to the entrance of our building, I found my sister Naomi jumping rope nearby.

"Don't you look great," she said. "You look like a wild man."

"It's none of your business," I answered her, and I went inside feeling rotten.

"You boys, you're all wild!" Naomi called after me.

I didn't answer her. It wasn't true, was it? There must be some boys who aren't wild...somewhere.

The next afternoon after school, we showed up on the hill with reinforcements. Not just us — them too.

The war continued full force. And it kept going until some adults from the shul nearby came out and yelled at us.

But the next day we fought again. I felt myself changing from a nice, quiet kid into a wild one. It seemed like my *yetzer ha-ra* had taken over. Taken over all of us. I barely recognized myself and the kids I used to know.

One day, when we all ran to the hill after school as usual, we saw that someone had put a fence around it. It was made of wood, and it was pretty high. But we ignored it; we just climbed over it and played inside. Or rather, we continued our war. By now we each knew our positions. There were kids in defense, and kids in charge of making the paper balls that we were throwing at each other. (We stopped throwing rocks after the second day, when one of the kids got a cut on his head.) There were even spies, and I was one of those.

The next day, we saw a bulldozer inside the fence. A sign had been hung from a tree: DANGER! CONSTRUCTION SITE. We tried to climb in anyway, but there were some workers there who chased us away.

Naftali said, "Oh, no, they're putting up a

building. There'll be no place left to play." Little by little, both sides gathered and glumly watched that bulldozer begin ruining our hill.

"It's all Hillel's fault," announced Nachum. "Hashem is punishing us because of him."

"Yeah, and you didn't fight too?" asked Dovid. "Look who's talking."

So we were back to our war.

Days passed, and we could only stand by helplessly and watch our hill being flattened chunk by chunk.

One evening, after *Ma'ariv*, when all the kids had gone home, I saw there was a full moon shining down on our hill. I climbed over the fence to look around at our favorite old playing field — where I had spent so many happy times.

Now there was only destruction — piles of broken rocks and our favorite climbing tree uprooted and broken on the ground. I felt so sad. I couldn't even find an anthill left untouched. I looked at the bulldozer that had caused all this ruin, and I felt so angry that I wanted to kick the big thing, to punish it for what it had done.

But right away I realized that I was just being silly. And I realized that if I wanted to get angry, I could get plenty angry at myself for how I and my friends had been acting.

Then my eye suddenly fell on something familiar. It was a piece of a big chalk rock that was now in pieces. Once, a long time ago, we had engraved the words "CHILDREN'S HILL" on it. I picked up the piece. It just said, "CHILDREN'" …the rest of it was gone.

I stared at the rock and I felt tears come to my eyes. Suddenly I heard a sound behind me. I turned around. It was Nachum. He was looking at me, without saying a word. I could see that he was holding a piece of rock in his hand just like the piece I had in my hand.

We started walking towards each other. I held out my piece of rock with the word "CHILDREN'" on it. Nachum nodded, and his eyes lit up. He held out the piece he was holding and fit it against mine. It was like a jigsaw puzzle. We had put "CHILDREN'S HILL" together again.

Silence.

"It's too late now," I heard myself say, and I sighed.

"Maybe not," Nachum answered.

"What do you mean?" I asked him, surprised. "Do you think something can still be done?"

"Yes, I do," he said. "My father works for the city. He says this area is marked as a 'green area' on the city plans. It's supposed to be a park, not a building."

"Really?" I said, feeling hopeful for the first time, and even a little happy. "So why doesn't he hurry up and tell those people that they have to stop building here?"

"My father's not willing to go to the trouble," answered Nachum sadly. "He says he has no interest in saving our battlefield."

I couldn't think of an answer to that. I just kept quiet.

Nachum continued, "He's right, isn't he? I mean, why should he put himself out to help us fight some more?"

"Listen, Nachum," I said, "I have an idea. Let's sit down together and write a letter promising that we will never again fight over this hill, and let's send it to your father."

Nachum thought about it and said, "That's a good idea." We each went home.

The next day during recess, Nachum came up to my classroom, and together we sat down and wrote out a really nice letter. All the other kids stood around us, surprised to see that sworn enemies could sit together like that. When they read the letter, they understood. Everyone signed, then we sent the letter off to the city, to Nachum's father's office.

Another week passed and we were all tense, hoping to see something change. But the bulldozers kept working. We were so disappointed. Then the following week, the work stopped! And for two whole weeks, no work was done on our hill. We knew something must be happening in the offices of the city government.

It was about a month later that people came and took away the machinery and the sign announcing the new building. But they left the fence up.

A week after that, different bulldozers, with the city emblem on them, came instead. They started to work, and they worked fast. In a few weeks, they built a gigantic playground — with a big, smooth ball field and lots of new equipment to play on.

I heard a voice coming from the new field, announcing out loud: "Whoever wants to play ball, come over here! Hillel and I are choosing teams."

I have to say, I still miss the old hill with all the rocks, and those bushes, and those anthills. But when I hear the happy voices of my friends and of the younger kids, who forgot all about the war, I realize that the only thing we really gave up was our battlefield.

And — don't you agree? — that's not much of a loss.

My name is Chananel, and I'm in the fifth grade. One day in school my finger got stuck in one of the holes in my desk. (There's lots of holes that kids have made over the years in the wooden desks.) I couldn't pull my finger out. The principal had to come in and he tried pouring some dishwashing soap on my finger so it would slip out, but it didn't work.

So we went down to the floor where the teachers' room is. We went with the desk, the teacher and the principal holding the desk from each side, and me in the middle stuck in the desk! Boy was that embarrassing. We went into the teachers' room, and the principal brought in this big saw, and he tried but he couldn't. That minute the bell rang for recess, and all the teachers came into the room. The kids were standing outside the door and trying to peek through the keyhole and through any hole they could find. All the teachers were trying their ideas, and NOTHING worked. One of the teachers felt sorry for me and he brought me something to drink. I looked so silly.

From the minute the teachers walked in, the jokes didn't stop. One of the teachers said he guessed I'd just have to go home with the desk. That made me happy because I knew my family would manage to get my finger out and then we'd have an extra desk!

Finally one of the teachers came in with a big screwdriver and a hammer, and he banged in the screwdriver near one side of my hand, and then near the other side. My finger came o
But we lost the desk.

Yours,
Chananel

When Bad Luck
is Good Luck

My name is Chaya and I'm a fifth-grader. I'm not one of the better students in my class. In fact, they say I'm lazy.

I'm not dumb. Really I'm not. It's just that I've never liked school or studying, so I've never wanted to work at it.

My mother is totally diferent. She's always reading — always interested in learning something new. When she was little, they called her a bookworm. And of course, she always did great in school. I heard all this stuff from my grandmother, who's so proud of her daughter. I just hope she doesn't know how it is with me, her granddaughter.

Anyway, listen to what happened to me. I fell one day, right in the schoolyard, and broke my leg in two separate places. They put a big cast on my leg, and told me I had to stay in bed for a few weeks before I could start walking around with crutches. What rotten luck, right?

After a few days, it stopped hurting me so much. I just had to rest with the cast on and not move around. I thought I really had it made. I mean, what could be better for a lazy girl like me than being told to rest?

I stayed in bed and I was thrilled that I didn't have to go to school. Also, because the teacher had heard I was in a lot of pain, she didn't send me any work to do at home. So I didn't have to do homework or study for tests or anything!

But, do you know what? After a week, I have to admit I started getting bored. I mean, how long can you lie in bed without friends to play with or anything to do? Can you believe it, I even started to miss schoolwork!

I was so bored, I started paying attention to the only thing going on in the house: my mother's work.

I forgot to tell you what my mother does. She types stories and books and stuff into a computer. She sits at the computer screen most of the day, looks at some pages, and types whatever is written on them.

It's fun to watch the letters racing across the screen at such a high speed. My mother is one fast typist. She once told me that she can type nearly a hundred words a minute. That is FAST! Who can even *say* a hundred words in one minute?

One day my mother asked, "Chaya, would you mind proofreading this story?"

"Proofreading?" I asked. "What's that?"

"That means to read through the story for mistakes and see if I spelled any words wrong, or put commas in the wrong place, and to make sure that I put a period at the end of every sentence. Things like that. You may find some really big mistakes. Because I type so quickly, I never catch my own mistakes."

I took the pages she had printed out and I started looking them over. Now, you have to understand that I am a rotten speller and I'm no whiz at punctuation either. So at first I figured I didn't have much of a chance of doing a good job. I mean, how would I be able to find spelling mistakes? Still, I started to read.

It was a story about a boy traveling on a ship around eighty years ago. The ship had a hard name: The Titanic. The boy was traveling with his father.

"Father," I said out loud.

"What?" my mother asked. "Your father's not home."

"I know, I know," I laughed. "But you wrote 'fother' with an *o* instead of an *a.*"

"Oh, it's great that you found that mistake." She put a little X in the margin and wrote "father."

I read on. The boy was traveling with his father and thousands of travelers, and they were all really, really rich. The Titanic was a "luxur ship," it said.

"What does 'luxur' mean?" I asked my mother.

"Oh, good for you, Chaya," said my mother. "You found another mistake. The word should be 'luxury.' Do you know what that means?"

Sure, that I knew. "Fancy, with all kinds of nice things."

The passengers on the ship were so proud of themselves because they were on the largest ship ever, and it was also supposed to be the safest ship that had ever sailed the seas. (While reading this I noticed that there was a period that had made its way into the middle of a sentence, and that one time the word "ship" was missing an *i*.)

The story was so interesting I felt I couldn't stop reading. But it was so sad. It turned out that the ship rammed into an iceberg (What's an iceberg? A huge mountain of ice floating in the sea) and started to sink. It tipped over on its side (the word can't be "sode," it must be "side") and water started flooding (it can't be "glooding") the deck. Then pandemonium broke out. I didn't know that word, so I asked my mother.

"Pandemonium means panic and confussion," she explained.

That made sense. People started rushing toward the lifeboats. But there weren't enough of them on board, because no one expected this ship to sink.

The boy writing the story survived, but his father didn't. He drowned, along with fifteen hundred other men and women.

It was so sad. But what a gripping story it was.

"Is this story true?" I asked my mother.

"Of course," she answered. Didn't you ever read about the Titanic?"

I shrugged. Me? When was I ever interested in reading anything?

"Do you have another story for me?" I asked my mother.

"Sure," she said, and she handed me one every bit as exciting, about an atom bomb that was dropped on a city called Hiroshima in Japan. This was also a very sad story and, unfortunately, also a true one. In the second story I found lots of little mistakes.

In the next few days, I read more stories that my mother worked on, and I marked all the mistakes that I found. Time passed and I began discovering a magical world that I had never known was there. I suddenly understood how much I had been missing. There were so many things I could have known if only I had read more. I started to think that it doesn't pay to be lazy.

A month passed. Because I was spending so much time correcting my mother's typing, I decided it would be a good idea to look over the grammar and spelling books we had used in the third and fourth grade, so I could do a better job. I had all the rules memorized in a few days. I knew them so well that I felt I would get an "Excellent" on a grammar test if I took one now. (I don't remember ever getting even a "Good" on a grammar test.)

My mother gave me a dictionary too, so I could look up words if I wasn't sure how to spell them. Now I've gotten to the point where I can correct nearly every mistake in spelling, grammar, and punctuation. Nearly, I say, because there are still some things I miss. My mother points them out to me afterwards.

That's it, kids. Soon I'll be able to walk and go back to school. Next week, the doctor said. I can't believe this myself, but I actually am counting the days until I can go back. Not because I know that I have to, but because now I really, really want to.

I know that being at home with your leg in a cast is not supposed to be a good thing. But my situation turned out to have a silver lining for me. I discovered a whole new world that I know I will enjoy from now on.

World's Most Miserable Champ

My name's Aharon and I'm in the seventh grade. It's very late, but I can't sleep. I'm sad — I'm so unhappy.

First, I should tell you that just this evening, I won the title of "Mishnah Champion" in our school. It was a big contest, held in the school auditorium in front of all the kids. There were 10 of us boys on the stage, chosen from the 600 students in the school because we did the best in the *Mishnayos* Campaign.

So why am I sad? I'm one of the smartest kids in the class. I'm not the only smart kid — there are a few as smart as me — but for some reason, the kids like them and not me.

I've been a top student ever since first grade. My report card always showed the best marks. But nobody ever liked me.

It could be that some of it's my own fault. I like to show how much I know, and maybe sometimes it's at another kid's expense. If someone gets stuck in the middle of an answer, I raise my hand right away to show that I know the answer better.

When they announced the *Mishnayos* Campaign, I spent all my days and nights studying for it. During recess, instead of going out to play, I reviewed *mishnayos.* When I got home from school, I did my homework, and then I stayed up late in order to memorize the Bartenuras, too.

I got 100 on the first test, so I was able to enter the second level. There were 120 boys who reached that level. Then there was a harder test, and only 20 of us reached the finals.

The big playoff started in the afternoon in the school auditorium, in front of all the kids in the whole school. The men asking the questions came from outside our school. There were three parts to the contest. First, they asked each kid a question. Whenever the kid answered, he got lots of applause from the audience. Even if his answer wasn't so great.

They applauded my answer also. But I saw that not everybody was clapping for me. Some kids weren't so interested in giving me encouragement. Those were the kids from my class.

Then the second stage of the playoff started. There were only ten of us on the stage. The whole thing happened all over again: Every student got lots of encouragement from the audience. I did too, but...

This "but" really hurt my feelings. I could see that the kids in my class preferred Heshy and Shaulie over me. Whenever they answered, the whole class stood up and clapped for a long time.

Then the second stage was over, and the five boys who would take part in the final playoff were called up to the stage. There was Yehuda from the eighth grade, Pinny and Shlomo from the sixth, and Shaulie and me from the seventh.

Shaulie is also one of the smartest kids in the class. He's a good boy, with really good *middos*. I like him a lot.

The final playoff began — there were two questions for each contestant. I'll never forget what happened then. The kids in my class started to roar: "Shaulie! Shaulie!" to cheer him on, even when it wasn't his turn.

I felt awful, but I tried to tell myself it wasn't so bad. "What's wrong with their cheering him?" I asked myself. "He's a good kid, and everyone likes him, and they'd be happy if he won."

But then when I answered my question and received 20 points (that was the maximum number of points you could get), I could see the disappointment written on their faces. In fact, one boy, whose name I won't write, actually said out loud, "Oh, phooey!" It was really hard for me to keep from crying, but I told myself just to concentrate on the contest.

The first round of questions was over, and by then everyone knew that Yehuda, Pinny, and Shlomo wouldn't be able to win because they hadn't gotten the full number of points. Then came the last question. The same question was given to all of us and we were asked to write our answers on a piece of paper.

The tension was tremendous. The kids from my class were already standing on their chairs, screaming: "Shaulie! Shaulie!" The principal made them get down and be quiet, but it didn't matter anymore. The whole school already knew who they wanted to win.

I kept on writing my answer to the hard question — it had lots of quotes from different *mishnayos*. We finished our answers and the judges began checking them. The whole auditorium was in an uproar of shouts for Shaulie. There's just no way to describe to anyone how I felt during those long minutes. I was all red, and I wished the earth would open up and swallow me — I was so sorry I had ever entered the contest. I could've learned all these *mishnayos* for myself, I thought, without having to go through this terrible embarrassment.

Shaulie didn't look too comfortable either. He was sitting right next to me, and you could see the tension on his face.

Suddenly, I felt his hand on my shoulder. "Don't pay any attention to them," he said. "They're making noise for no good reason."

What a nice kid. "Oh, it's okay," I said. But it wasn't.

The judges finished. The principal walked over to the microphone. "In third place we have Pinny Shapiro, eighth grade. He is the second deputy to the Mishnah Champion!" The eighth graders clapped and shouted deafening cheers.

"In second place..." There was absolute silence in the hall. Every eye was on the principal's mouth. Once we knew who was in second, we'd know who the champion was.

"Shaulie Solomon," announced the principal.

"PHOO!" was the sound that followed that announcement, until a few seconds passed and some boys remembered that they should be applauding.

"And in first place, Mishnah Champion for this year, is Aharon Levinsky!"

The dramatic tone of the principal's voice didn't help. The clapping in the audience was weak, and the sound of people whispering and talking to each other was louder.

Shaulie got up and shook my hand warmly. I stood up to walk over to the principal and get the prize. But my eyes filled with tears, and they started rolling down my face. I just wanted to disappear.

The contest ended, and I wanted to run home as fast as my feet would carry me. I was all alone. Almost. You know who came with me? Shaulie.

It seems the other kids wanted to lift him up and carry him around as if he were the champ, and he wouldn't hear of it. Instead, he attached himself to me and said, "Come on, Aharon, let's go home."

We walked quietly the whole way. I couldn't speak. I was crying silently the entire time.

When we got to my house, Shaulie said, "Don't be so sad. I mean, you *are* the champ. You should be happy."

I looked at him and I said, "I can see why all the kids wanted you to be the winner. You really deserve a title...something better than Mishnah Champion. I appreciate the way you've treated me. I also feel bad that you didn't win."

"Thanks," said Shaulie, and he waved his hand and headed to his house.

Now it's really late, and I still can't fall asleep. I feel so miserable.

I know I've made a lot of mistakes and I'm going to start correcting them tomorrow. But I'm sure that what the other kids did to me today was also a big mistake. They embarrassed me. They embarrassed me in front of the whole school!

I hope they're planning to change their behavior. Like me.

Alone

My name is Tammy. I'm in the fourth grade. I'm a chubby girl, and, until recently, I was not a very good girl either. Rather difficult, I'd even say.

I'm not like the other girls. They're always sweet and good, trying to do their work carefully and all that stuff. But, me — I goof off and misbehave a lot.

The truth is, I'm not so dumb. I mean, whenever I decide to pay attention in class, I catch on to what the teacher's saying right away.

I just never feel like paying attention. I always sit in the last row. By myself. Don't think that is where the teacher puts me. I always find that seat for myself at the beginning of the year.

Teachers try to talk me into moving, but I refuse, and sooner or later they just decide to leave me alone.

They also try putting other girls near me, but

I always bother them and — one after another — they ask to have their seats changed. This goes on for a while, until no girl in my class is willing to sit next to me.

Now, you're probably going to ask me why I do this. I have no idea. That's just how I am.

During recess, I play by myself — with a ball or a jump rope. I almost never include anyone else in my games. The truth is that the other girls asked me to join them a few times, and I did, but then I just bothered them until they got sick and tired of me. That's how I would upset all the girls, until not one was left who was interested in me. And you know what? I don't care one bit.

Every once in awhile, a teacher comes up to me and asks why I stay away from all the others — why I cut myself off from them.

"They keep away from *me*," I answer with a shrug. But in my heart I know the truth.

One day we had a school trip to an amusement park. As usual, I sat down in the back seat of the bus and didn't let anyone sit next to me. It wasn't much of a problem — I mean, no one exactly asked to sit with me.

When we arrived at the amusement park, all of us ran to the rides. I loved it. First, I rode the train, then the airplanes, and after that I spent a lot of time on the bumper cars. Then I went back to the train. I just played and played. There wasn't anybody else with me, but I didn't care.

Hours went by, and I was still running back and forth from line to line to get onto one ride or the other.

When I got off the airplanes for the fourth time, I suddenly saw my teacher. She looked really upset, and the inside corners of her eyes were wet.

"Where were you?" she asked sharply.

"What do you mean? I was on the rides," I answered.

"Didn't you hear us paging you on the loud-speaker?" she asked.

"No."

"Do you know how long the buses waited for you?" she asked me.

I answered, "No."

"We have been searching for you for an entire hour, with all the girls waiting on the buses. Fifteen minutes ago, I told the drivers to take the students and teachers back to school, and I would stay behind alone to look for you."

Boy. I just kept quiet. I didn't know what to say.

The teacher took my hand and led me to the exit, where several security men were standing.

"It's okay," she told them. "I found her."

One of them asked her, "How can you bring such an irresponsible child to a big place like this?"

She didn't answer him, but she sure gave me a long, angry look. Then she hailed a taxi and told him where to take us.

In the taxi, neither one of us spoke a word. Then my teacher began, "I want you to explain something to me, Tammy. For a full hour, you did not see a single one of your classmates. But you kept going on the rides. How could you be so lost in your own world?"

I kept quiet.

"Do you think it's normal for a ten-year-old girl to think nothing of being all alone in such a large place? Any other girl would have been worried and looking everywhere for at least one other familiar face."

I still kept quiet.

"Tammy, maybe the time has come for you to admit that you have a problem. You cannot go on like this."

"What problem?" I asked, surprised.

"Don't you realize that your behavior is very different from all the other girls?"

I thought a minute, and then I just nodded.

The teacher looked at me and asked, "Maybe you can tell me exactly how you are different from your classmates?"

I couldn't. I mean, I knew, but I couldn't say it in words.

"You are cut off from the whole world. You have no interest in anyone around you. Do you really have no need for any friends?"

"I need them. I need them very much!" I suddenly heard myself scream.

"Well, then how do you explain your behavior?" the teacher asked.

I had no answer. I really couldn't figure that one out myself.

"Would you be interested in playing with the others?"

"Yes," I whispered.

"Do you sometimes feel lonely?"

"Always," I answered. "But the others don't really like me very much."

"Do you have an explanation for that?"

"Y...yes. I think there's an explanation."

"Would you like me to help you become friends with the others?" asked the teacher.

"Yes," I said.

"All right, then. Starting tomorrow, you will do exactly what I tell you to do. Agreed?"

"Agreed," I said.

The next day the teacher moved me to the front row. She seated me next to Shoshie, a smart, good girl. At first we weren't so comfortable next to each other. Then, Shoshie asked me if I could lend her my eraser. That broke the ice. Then, I asked her if I could borrow her red pen. I didn't need it, but I wanted an excuse to talk to her.

At recess, Shoshie asked me to join her game. The teacher had warned me that if I was invited to play, I should always agree. So I joined in. At first, the other girls looked at me very suspiciously. But when they saw that this time I wasn't bothering them, they just relaxed and let me play like the rest.

Days have passed since then. I'm lots less lonely now. I have some friends. Shoshie has already come to my house. I've also been to hers. And I'm even doing better in school.

I can't really explain to you why I kept away from kids for so long, and why I chose loneliness instead. It's not clear to me in my own mind. But I thought I should tell you my story so that you could see how I did manage to get out of it, even without understanding it. Maybe you have the same problem, or maybe there's someone in your class like me.

Loneliness is very hard. Even if you know someone who seems really interested in being alone — believe me, it would be a nice idea to try to get her — or him — out of it.

Identical and Different

My name is Gadi. I live in Bnei Brak, and I'm in the fifth grade. The story that I'm going to tell you is one that I never told before.

There are twenty-two boys in my class, and I get along just great with all of them — except one. His name is Gideon. His nickname is Giddi.

Giddi is one of the best boys in the class. He's very smart, and everybody likes him, but I still don't get along with him.

Oh. I forgot to mention something. Giddi and I sort of look alike — actually, like two peas in a pod. Lots of people get us mixed up because we look so much alike! Still, I don't get along with him. Um…Giddi is my twin brother.

My mother tells me I'm actually five minutes older than he is. We are identical twins — absolutely identical. Our faces, the color of our hair and the way our hair grows — all identical. My mother says that when we were babies, she had to dress us in different clothes just so *she* could tell us apart and not feed the same baby twice! And even so, Imma says, she would get all mixed up lots of times and forget which baby was wearing what.

I once asked her, "Could it be you got mixed up and I'm really Giddi?" But she just laughed and said that she has her secret signs and she'll never get mixed up about which one is Gadi and which one is Giddi.

Well, little by little, we grew up. In the fourth grade, we both needed glasses and we got the exact same frames, so we ended up looking more identical than ever.

Our teachers could never be sure which one of us was Gadi and which was Giddi. At the beginning of the year, that is. But after a few months they would begin to see that Giddi was the serious one. He always did his homework and he always knew the answers. His marks were always among the best. And me — I always placed somewhere in the middle of the class.

So the teachers, one after another, began telling us apart more easily. It went like this: If one of us said he hadn't done his homework, the teacher would say, "You're Gadi, right?" Right. And he would put a bad mark next to my name.

I mean, it usually was me who hadn't done the homework. But still, it bothered me that they always guessed my name right away for something like that, and not my brother's.

As time passed, I found myself feeling more and more angry and jealous of Giddi. Whenever the teacher praised him, I was jealous. And if the teacher yelled at me for something, I felt so low.

So that's why he's the only kid in the class that I don't like, and sometimes can't stand. It really bugs me that my own identical twin — and five minutes younger than me, at that! — should be the smartie, and me the dummy, and that the teachers praise him while I get nothing.

Last night, I suddenly remembered that I hadn't prepared for Gemara class. When I told my mother, she said, "Giddi can help you."

"NO!" I screamed. "Enough! Enough! I can't stand it any more!"

My mother's eyes got big and round. I had screamed so loud that all my brothers and sisters ran into the kitchen to see what had happened. My father came in last. He gave me a really sharp look.

I'm a pretty good kid, and nobody in my house has ever heard me scream at my parents like that. I don't really know what came over me — I guess I just lost control.

"We don't say no to Imma," my father reminded me. "Why are you so angry?"

I kept quiet.

"Gadi, tell me," my father insisted. "What made you shout like that?" But I just kept my mouth shut.

Both my parents tried to get me to talk to them, but I finally walked away and went straight to bed. (Nope, I never did prepare for class.)

After that, my father kept trying to get out of me exactly what was making me so angry. I was sure that he already knew, and that he just wanted me to say the words myself. That's the kind of father he is. He always says, "Half the solution to any problem is telling the right person about it, and getting it out in the open."

Well, in the end I did get it out. The truth is that I wanted to talk about it, but I had some kind of wall inside stopping me. Finally I just climbed over it.

I told my father how I felt. Then he explained to me that everyone in the world is different from everyone else. No two people are equally as good at the same things, even if they're twins.

"Everyone must look at himself. Instead of comparing himself to others, he must try to see the good that's inside of him."

"But Abba," I wanted to know, "then why do

the teachers always compare me to Giddi? Even at home you say Giddi is better at things. It really hurts. Is it my fault that I'm not as smart as he is?"

My father didn't answer me for a minute. He was thinking. Then he said, "Gadi, you're right. It was a mistake for us to ever compare you to Giddi. But you should understand that it was never because anyone thought you weren't as good as he. We love you every bit as much as we love him. It's just that we always wanted you to try to do better in school, but we went about it in the wrong way."

My father quietly stroked my head for a while, and it felt good. Then he put his hand on my shoulder and he said, "Okay, from now on look at yourself and the good things you do without comparing yourself to your brother, and I will do the same."

The next day in school, I wondered to myself, What's to look at? It's just tests and homework day after day. But then our teacher surprised us by ending class ten minutes early.

"Okay," he said, "who will volunteer to plan our *Siyyum* Party for the end of the term?" We all raised our hands.

I couldn't believe it, but the teacher chose me. "You're Gadi, aren't you? Good. This is a perfect job for you."

I wasn't sure about that, but I was very happy. I chose a committee of five, and we met several times a week to decide what we were going to do and how we were going to do it.

Weeks later, our teacher paid me another compliment. He came to class with his hand on the shoulder of a new student, Chaim. After introducing him to us, the teacher wondered out loud, "Let's see, where would be a good place to put you? Oh, I know. Take the seat next to Gadi. He'll help you get settled in."

I kept busy working on the party, and I made sure that Chaim wasn't having any trouble with the school work and that boys were playing with him. I loved every minute of it.

Then the day of the *Siyyum* Party came, and it was a big success! Teachers and even the principal said they had never seen anything like it. I guess I must be good with people and at organizing things.

Even Chaim is doing well in school. The teacher told me so, and gave me a friendly slap on my back!

Now I feel proud of myself. I guess my father was right. I have my own things I'm good at, and I don't have to go comparing myself to Giddi. I mean, his marks are still much better than mine, but that's not something I should blame him for. He's just being himself, and now that

I know things I'm good at, I can work on being myself, too.

Little by little, I'm starting to be Giddi's friend. After all, he lives nearby and we have a lot in common, and most of all, I've come to love him like I love myself.

The Fib

My name is Tzippy, and I'm in the sixth grade.

Last year was a nightmare for me, but *baruch Hashem*, everything got straightened out in the end.

It was all because of a dumb mistake I made. You see, I have a very special group of friends. There's Chana, with her beautiful, long red hair. Raizy has a great singing voice, so warm and clear. Itta, well, she's the top student in the class. And Ruchi, my best friend, has a terrific sense of humor.

Compared to them, I'm nothing special. And I so wanted to be.

For weeks I thought of nothing besides how I could be outstanding in some way. I tried piano lessons. Who knows? Maybe I was really talented in music. But I wasn't — I didn't even like to practice. I tried to write poetry. Maybe I was good with words. But I sat with my pen in my hand and a blank sheet of paper in front of me for nearly two hours. I simply didn't have anything I wanted to say.

What could I be that would be special? I didn't know until it came to me in a flash while I was studying for a test in my bedroom with Ruchi. We were nearly finished when I leaned forward to her and whispered, "Ruchi, I just can't hold this in any longer. I've got to tell you. I think I'm adopted!"

"Adopted?" she answered. "What makes you say that?"

"Well," I replied, "I'm not at all like anyone else in my family, if you think about it. I'm the the only one with curly blond hair. Everyone else has straight, brown hair. My brothers and sisters all get terrific grades in school. Mine are okay, but nowhere near as good as theirs. Also, they're all short for their age, and I'm the third tallest girl in the class!

"I asked my mother about it and she just laughed and shook her head. She wouldn't even answer me!"

Ruchi looked at me and her eyes widened. "Neat!" she said. "Wait till I tell everyone."

The next day at school, my friends all stood around me, asking questions.

"Why don't you make your mother tell you?"

"Did you check your brothers' and sisters'

noses and mouths? In my family, that's where we all look alike."

"How do you feel about it?"

"Where do you think your real parents are?"

Suddenly I was special! Now I had a very important secret that only my good friends knew about. Somehow, my secret had made my whole group of friends feel excited and closer because it was something only we knew about. My fib had really paid off!

But then, after Pesach, the sky fell in. Our teacher, Mrs. Luban, assigned us a project to trace our family trees and gather as much information as we could about all our relatives. Then we were to make a ten-minute presentation in class about where we came from, famous people in our family tree, and which relative we thought we were most like. We were also supposed to bring in pictures of our parents when they were our age.

My mind started to race. This will not be a problem, I said to myself. It's only natural to report on my adoptive family's tree as if it were my own, so no one will think anything of it.

Which relative I am most like will be a little harder, because I told my friends that I'm different from everyone in my family. A twinge of guilt surrounded my heart, but I pushed it away. Well, I can say I'm most like one of my great-grandmothers. Neither one of them's still alive, so I can make up stuff about what they were like...

Suddenly a voice in my head asked, "Tzippy, what are you doing?"

"What am I doing?" I repeated. And then I thought about it. I was just trying to protect my original story. I could make up things about a dead relative and it wouldn't hurt anyone. And best of all, no one would know.

So I asked my mother if she could get me some old pictures of her and of my father. Both of my grandmothers were happy to lend them to her. First was Abba, looking so young and sweet. His hair was dark brown, not full of gray like it is now. And then there was Imma, looking...oh no, her hair was just like mine!

I asked her about it and she said, "It's really strange, but once I started covering my hair, it got darker and straighter."

So I was stuck. Once I showed that picture, all my friends would see how much I looked like my mother, and they would know I'd told a fib.

What should I do? I thought and I thought. Then I came up with an idea. I could say that we didn't have a picture of my mother from when she was my age because there had been a fire at my grandmother's house about ten years ago, and everything had been destroyed.

"What are you doing, Tzippy?" that same voice in my head practically shouted at me.

Then I realized — that fib was leading me to make up more and more stories. I had to stop it now, or it would never end.

A few days later, when Ruchi came over to study for our history test, I admitted to her what I'd done. "I just wanted to be special like you all are, so I told this little fib. Can you explain it to everyone for me?"

"Little fib?" she retorted. "That was no little fib. That was a big, fat lie! I'm angry at you! You misled me and I trusted you. I thought we were best friends. I can't forgive you for trying to fool me, and I don't think the other girls will either!"

Ruchi left right after that, without even studying with me.

The next day in school, my friends shot me dirty looks and refused to talk to me. I had to eat lunch alone and pretend at recess that nothing was wrong when they turned their backs on me. It went on that way for more than a month...until our family presentations began.

Most of the class gave their talks before mine, and they were really pretty interesting. Some of the girls are actually related to famous *tzaddikim*. Others had stories to tell about life in Europe before World War II, or some *middah* their relative was known for. It made me think about how important families are for us and how we should cherish one another.

When my turn came, I went up in front of the class and looked at each of my former friends. They were all focusing on something besides me, with angry expressions on their faces. I felt terrible.

I can't let this go on another minute, I decided. I began my presentation, "Before I tell you about my family, there's something else I have to say. A few months ago, I did a terrible *averah*. I told my good friends that I was adopted so that they would think I was something special, the way that I think they're all special. And it worked for a while. I got lots of attention and I felt like somebody.

"But then I began to realize that I hadn't just told them some harmless little fib. I had told them a big lie that needed more big lies to protect it.

"I hurt my friends by trying to fool them, I hurt my family by saying they weren't my real family, and most of all, I hurt myself. I have wonderful parents who love me, and that makes me special enough. I should have seen that from the beginning. So I'm begging my friends to forgive me for this terrible thing I did, and now let me show you some pictures and tell you about my family tree..."

Metal Mouth

My name is Yanky. I'm in the fourth grade.

I do okay in school and I'm pretty friendly, but I have a certain social problem. It has to do with my upper teeth. They stick out of my mouth in a funny way. When I close my mouth, my upper front teeth stay outside. They really ruin the way I look. I would be a good-looking kid, except those teeth make me look like an ugly kid. Also, I can't chew a toffee with my front teeth.

But the biggest problem is what I said before, the social problem. What do I mean by that? I hear a lot of remarks from kids about my teeth. It makes me think they're always looking at me, even when they aren't making remarks. Once a kid I didn't even know called me Bugs Bunny.

I was so embarrassed I cried. And I wondered how kids could be so mean.

One day my mother took me to an orthodon-

tist. He examined my mouth and said, "No problem. We just have to make him a Hawley brace."

No problem? Ha. And what's a Hawley brace?

First, they attached metal brackets to my teeth, to help push the teeth inward. Then I got this big metal kind of headband that was attached to a rubber thing so I could wear it around my face. I had to wear it a certain number of hours each day, to press my teeth back even harder.

Well, if I thought that my problem had been solved, I soon discovered that it had only just begun. From the first day I came to school with that weird-looking contraption around my head, and those brackets on my teeth, the number of remarks doubled. Or more than doubled.

I mean, I don't think there was a kid in the whole class who didn't have *something* to say to me. One boy kindly said, "Only girls walk around with those." Another looked in my mouth and said, "Oh, I see you decided to start eating metal." All in all, they found the brace an excuse to tease me more than ever.

Naturally, I started to hate the thing. Which — I haven't even told you yet — also hurt terribly because it pressed so hard against my teeth.

As soon as I got home each day, I would pull the horrible brace off my head to at least get some relief from the pain in my mouth.

Every night before going to sleep, I would have to clean those metal brackets pressing on my teeth. It was a tiring business getting all the food out of each of them. It took forever. But I had to do it every night or the dirt would just build up.

One morning I...um...forgot the brace at home. The next day, I "forgot" again. The third day, my mother stood by the door and said, "Here, take the brace, or you'll forget it again."

"I don't want to wear it, Imma," I told her.

"What? But why not?"

"Don't ask me why," I answered. "I just don't want to."

My mother looked at me and said, "I know it hurts your teeth, but for your own sake, you have to wear it."

We stood there in the doorway, my mother with the Hawley brace in her hand and I. I said, "If it only hurt my teeth, I would be willing to suffer. The problem is that it hurts my heart, too."

I ran off without the thing. I didn't want my mother to see me crying.

Days passed. My mother tried again to convince me to wear it, but I wouldn't budge. "I don't care," I kept repeating, "I am not wearing that thing again."

A few days ago, at recess, my teacher called

me into the teachers' lounge.

"What happened?" he asked me. "You were wearing a Hawley brace and now you stopped."

I didn't answer.

"It hurts, I know. Is that the reason?"

I nodded. But then I shook my head the other way.

The teacher copied my movements, and then made a funny circle with his head. "Well, is it yes or no?" he asked me.

"It's yes and no," I said.

"Is there another reason?" he asked.

"Yes."

"So what is it?"

I didn't answer that.

"You don't want to tell me," said the teacher. "So I'll tell you. But first I want you to take a look at me."

I looked. He pointed to his mouth. "Do you see my lower jaw?"

I looked. His lower teeth were pointed out. But they weren't exactly crooked like mine.

"I also had an orthodontia problem," he said. "My teeth were straight, but my jaw went forward at too much of an angle. Do you see?"

"Yes," I answered with interest.

"My mother took me to an orthodontist, and he gave me a rubber mask. It was designed to push my lower jaw backwards. When I put it on, it hurt terribly," the teacher said. "But the pain didn't bother me at all. I was so happy that my jaw would go back to a normal position, like everyone else's."

"But…" I began.

"But you see that it was not corrected, right?"

"Right."

"Well, let me tell you what happened. I started wearing it to school, and one day, a boy ran by me in the schoolyard and yelled, 'It's the masked boy!' And from then on, others called me that, and soon they were all calling me 'the masked boy.'"

"So what did you do?" I asked.

"I did what you did," replied the teacher. "I stopped wearing that mask. Do you think I did a smart thing?" When he asked me the question, the teacher was pointing to his jaw.

"No," I said, "but…"

"I know, I know," the teacher finished, "but what can you do? The kids make fun — right?"

"Yes," I said sadly.

"If I had only had the patience and strength to stand their laughter for a few months the way I was able to stand the pain," said the teacher, "I would have a normal-looking jaw today. Now you have to make your own decision."

The teacher slapped me fondly on the shoulder and walked out.

Um, so you want to know what I decided, right? Well, today, I finally put the weird thing back on. I guess I can take whatever I have to take. I just don't want to spend my whole life with these front teeth sticking out this way, and that's all there is to it.

My name is Yitzchak Mordechai and I'm a Kohen. Since I was born a short time after my grandmother's father died, I'm named after him.

My grandmother loves me a whole lot. Sometimes when she looks at me, her eyes fill up with tears, because she remembers her father who she loved a lot.

Do you know what she calls me? Abba'leh. Every time she comes to our house, she asks, "How's everybody?" And then she says,

"And where's my Abba'leh?"

בס״ד

y name is Sorale. When my mother told me to go out d play, I went out to play. Then a strange thing happened. car came into the yard of the building and it hit me and t hurt so so much and everybody all around was so quiet because everybody was scared and in a few minutes an ambulance came to help and take me to the hospital and there they made me better and I came home fine and my parents were very happy and so was I happy and so was the whole family happy and we all thanked Hashem for being so so good to me. And I learned that you can't just play wildly outside and you have to always look and see if a car is coming because it's really dangerous to play wildly and I learned that you can't cross alone—only if a man or a woman comes to cross you—so from now on I only cross with a man or a woman and that way it isn't dangerous, so you have to wait till a man or a woman comes.

Best wishes from Sorale.

Very Funny, But...

My name is Nechama, and I'm in the third grade. Would you believe that last week I almost died laughing? I know it sounds like a joke, but when you hear my story, I don't think you'll find it funny.

A couple of weeks ago, one of the girls in our class started jerking around and laughing hard at the same time. We didn't know what was so funny or why she was twisting and turning until we saw that there was someone behind her tickling her. She just kept tickling, and her friend kept laughing until she managed to run away.

Well, the other girls must have thought it was a great idea, because all that week, that's what they kept doing to each other during recess. Girls would grab other girls and start tickling them. It seemed like fun...all that laughing and everything. We never for a minute thought that something bad could come from it. And no one ever complained to the teacher — even though the girl being tickled usually didn't like it.

Then, one day, I was playing jacks. Chani and Gila sneaked up behind me and both began tickling me at once. I started laughing and twisting, trying to get away from them.

I said, "Leave me alone!" and "Stop, please stop!" But they saw I was laughing, so they kept going. They tickled my neck and my waist and under my arm...

Soon I started feeling sick. I was laughing, but I said, "Stop, please, please stop..."

They kept it up. Slowly, I felt my strength leaving me. Then I couldn't breathe. Then I felt nothing.

I woke up in the emergency room. Some doctors and nurses were bent over me, looking kind of worried.

Then one of them told me I had laughed so hard that I lost consciousness. "You're very lucky," the doctor explained. "The girls who were tickling you ran and called a teacher who knew first aid. She started you breathing again and took care of you until the ambulance came. You're going to have to stay here for a few hours so we can be sure you're okay."

I could tell my parents were very upset about what had happened, but really, it was only a game. Chani and Gila hadn't meant to hurt me.

I went back to school the next day, and all my friends crowded around me. Chani took my hand.

"What a stupid game that was," she said. "I'm really sorry." Gila nodded her head and looked like she was going to cry.

Later in the week, the school nurse came around to speak to all the classes. She told them all what had happened to me, and to some other girls, from dangerous games.

"You have to think before you play these games," she said. "Ask yourself if anything bad can happen in them, or, if someone looks un-happy while she's playing, stop at once."

So that's my story. Who'd think that a silly game could hurt anyone? Well, it's not the end of the world... There are plenty of other games we can play that don't hurt anyone, don't you think?

Latchkey Kid

My name is Meir, and I'm in the fifth grade. I'm what is called a "latchkey kid," and I want to tell you something about what that means, in case you don't know.

A latchkey kid is a kid who has to open the front door himself when he comes home from school — because there isn't anyone inside to open it for him. Some kids have their key hanging on a string around their necks. Mine is inside my book bag.

Maybe you don't understand why there isn't anyone home when I get there. It's simple: my father works until late at night, and my mother comes home from work late in the afternoon.

I finish my morning classes at one o'clock. My school is fairly close to the house, so I walk home and it takes me fifteen minutes. At a quarter past one I come home, open the door, and make a simple lunch for my brothers and myself. It's

usually something my mother has left for us in the refrigerator.

In a way, my sister and my two younger brothers are also latchkey children. Only they don't have keys. My mother is afraid that they would lose the key if she gave them one. I'm the only one she trusts. So sometimes they have to wait a few minutes for me until I get home to open the door for them.

When I open that door and everyone runs in, the fun starts!

First, I have to help Yitzie and Zevie take their coats off. Then I seat them at the table and serve them lunch. Sometimes a fight breaks out between my sister and one of my little brothers, and I have to calm things down. That's when I remember those good old days before I was a latchkey kid.

Before I started the fourth grade, my mother was home all day long. It was so good to come home and have a mother there to open the door for me, talk to me, and ask me how I was doing in school.

But it's okay. I mean, there's no choice. My mother says she has to work, or we wouldn't have enough money. I don't blame her.

At a quarter to three I have to go back to school for my afternoon classes. That's when I "hand the house over" to my sister Ruthie, who's in fourth grade. But not for very long, only about an hour. By four o'clock my mother comes home.

So that's the way it is every day. I'm used to it, and it's fine. But sometimes something happens that's hard for me to handle. Once I had to call an ambulance. That was when Yitzie ran up the stairs so fast that he fell and his chin hit the step. He cut himself and a lot of blood came pouring out. I didn't know what to do. Then I thought to call an ambulance. The phone number was right by our telephone. My mother had told me that if someone ever gets really sick or hurts himself badly, I should first call an ambulance and then call her.

The whole time, Yitzie was screaming his head off. And pretty soon, Ruthie and Zevie joined in. I mean, I wanted to cry too, but I was too busy.

The doctors jumped off the ambulance and kept asking me where my mother or father were. I told them: "My mother and father are at work, but I called my mother and she'll be home soon." I couldn't understand why they were saying over and over again, "You are terrific!" and "What a mature little boy you are."

They glued the cut together, and they bandaged him up right there. He didn't have to go to the hospital, *baruch Hashem.*

As soon as they left, I needed to cry hard, and that's exactly what I did.

My brothers looked at me in amazement.

"Why are you crying?" asked Yitzie.

Zevie added, "You acted just like Abba, and Abba never cries."

"Yes, I know," I answered them. "But I'm younger than Abba and these things scare me just like they scare you."

"So why weren't you crying when the rest of us did?" asked Ruthie, who had only then managed to calm down.

I tried to think of an answer to her question. Then it came to me. I took out my key to the house and said, "This is why."

Thanks to a Strict Teacher

My name is Sara and I'm a third-grader who's in the fourth grade. You must be wondering how that could be. Wait and I'll explain the whole thing so you won't have to wonder.

Last year I finished second grade, and I went on to third. At the beginning of the year, I managed to do my work somehow. But then I just stopped. I started fooling around in class and bothering the teacher. At first, the teacher spoke nicely to me, trying to understand what made me lose interest in my studies. But I didn't have any answer for her, and so she ended up shrugging her shoulders and walking away.

I really wanted to answer, but I couldn't. How could I tell her the real reason — that things at home were really tense and that it made me too nervous to pay attention? I wanted to tell her, but I couldn't. It didn't seem right.

Since I wasn't listening in class, I had nothing to do there. So I started playing little tricks. I would make paper airplanes and throw them just when they would make the biggest disturbance.

At first, the teacher asked me nicely to stop; then she asked me angrily. When nothing helped, she sent me to the principal's office.

The principal kept punishing me, time after time. But that didn't stop me either — I just kept disturbing the class whenever and however I could.

Finally, the teacher decided that every time I disturbed the class, she would ask me to leave the classroom. Soon, I was spending entire days out in the hall. It was even more boring for me outside the classroom than inside, so I would walk out to the drinking fountain in the school-yard and play with the water. I sprayed the water in all directions, even straight at myself.

When I got tired of playing with the water and I was soaked to the skin, I would play in the sandbox. Sand would then stick to my wet blouse until I looked like a sand cake.

This went on for weeks. When I walked home, no one would walk with me. I mean, that's not surprising, is it? Can you imagine walking with someone who looked like she just got swept in from a desert storm?

And when I walked through the door, my mother would shake her head in dismay, and make me go clean up immediately. The whole time she would say over and over, "Sara, why? Why do you do this to me? Don't I have enough on my hands?" And sometimes she even burst into tears.

What could I say to her? My problem was at home, but I didn't think my mother could fix it. I was mixed up and I just didn't want to talk about it.

More than once, my mother was called to school to speak with the principal. Each time, the principal called me into her office afterwards and told me, in front of my mother, "I spoke with your mother, Sara, and I want you to know that you are causing her a lot of grief. We have decided that you must promise to behave yourself." Then my mother and the principal would sit there and talk about me, about how bad I was and what punishments they would have to give me if I kept this up, and how good it would be for me if I started to behave.

So I promised each time that I would change. And my promise would last about one day. The next day, I would go right back to disturbing, being sent out, playing with water, then sand...

Once the principal called me to her office and there were some people there I didn't know.

Psychologists, she said. They asked me a lot of really weird questions. What business was it of theirs anyway? What I did was I answered in a few words that didn't say much, or else I didn't answer at all. I just kept my mouth shut.

This went on for half a year. Then, one day when I was rolling around in the sand, all wet and dirty, I felt a hand on my shoulder. I looked up and it was Mrs. Halevy, the fourth grade teacher.

I've always been afraid of Mrs. Halevy. She looks strict and angry. She has eyes that look straight through you. You feel really uncomfortable when she turns those eyes on you.

I stood up. I faced her without even brushing myself off. I mean, even if I had brushed myself off for half an hour I still would have been filthy, so why bother?

She fixed those eyes of hers on me and examined me from head to toe. I could see a mixture of amazement and anger on her face, with even a little pity thrown in.

"Now you listen to me, Sara," she said after a moment's silence. "You are going home this minute, washing up, and changing into clean clothes. Then you are coming back to me. Is that clear?"

"O...okay," I answered, because I was really afraid of her.

"Run!" she said harshly. And I ran.

My mother was surprised to see me in the middle of the day. The dirt and the sand were no surprise, of course, but at ten o'clock?

At half past ten I was back in school, washed, combed, and wearing fresh clothing.

I went to the school secretary, who told me that Mrs. Halevy was in the principal's office. Before I knocked at the principal's door, I could hear Mrs. Halevy's voice: "If you tell me that she has a high level of intelligence and comprehension, then she should be able to meet the challenge."

I assumed they were talking about me, and I didn't know what those words meant. They sounded like something bad.

I knocked and the principal said to come in. Mrs. Halevy fixed her eyes on me again. Then she softened a little bit and said, "Now we can talk to you, Sara, not when you look like a sand cake."

I laughed, but her face remained serious.

"You were a good student in first and second grade," she said to me. It wasn't a question, it was a statement. But I answered, yes.

"Suddenly, you got sloppy," she stated. I nodded.

"Something happened this year, right?"

"Right," I answered.

"Will you tell me what happened?" she asked me.

I didn't answer that at all.

She said,"It's hard for you to say it, right?"

I kept quiet.

"I'll help you," said Mrs. Halevy. "Does it have to do with your friends?"

I shook my head no.

"Does it have to do with your teacher?"

"No."

"With your family?"

I didn't answer, so she asked again, "Does it have something to do with your family?" I burst out crying.

"Sara, listen to me," she said. (She was always saying "listen to me.") "From today on you're in the fourth grade."

"WHAT?" I thought I had heard wrong.

"You will take your book bag — if you even have one — and come to my classroom. From today on, you will be in my class."

It seemed awfully strange to me, but there was no way I was going to argue. I went down to my classroom to get my book bag, and then I walked up to the fourth grade classroom.

When I got inside, Mrs. Halevy turned and pointed for me to sit in the second row. "Take the third seat," she said, just like I was one of the kids in her class from the beginning of the year having her seat changed.

I sat down, and Mrs. Halevy started teaching. Every once in a while, she would glance my way to see if I was paying attention. I was. Did I have a choice?

Afterwards, the teacher wrote some questions on the blackboard and she told me to copy them. As the day went on, I felt myself somehow getting used to fourth grade. And, what was really special, the girls in the class all acted very nice to me.

When I got home, I sat down to do my homework. It was the first time in six months. Don't think I did the homework because I wanted to. I was just terrified of this teacher. When I looked at the questions, I was amazed to see that I knew the answers. Within half an hour I had finished homework in three subjects.

That was the beginning. The days and weeks passed and — I don't know how — I became a good student. I was able to handle fourth-grade studies. I did my homework in a neat handwriting, and I even got good marks on tests.

All the while, Mrs. Halevy kept her eye on me. Every once in a while, she would call me over for a little talk. I did not want to cooperate with her, but she managed somehow to pull out of me the reason why I hadn't been able to concentrate on my schoolwork. I'm not going to tell you about it, because it's a secret, but she helped me a lot. She gave me some ideas; I tried them and they helped.

If I talked during class, Mrs. Halevy was very strict with me. But if I did something well, she made sure to praise me in front of everyone. In fact, once, she picked me up and seated me on top of a cabinet, as if I were somebody very special. Everybody laughed and clapped, and so did I.

Now, the truth is that I missed the girls in my class. They were my own age, and no matter what, I felt more comfortable with them. But when I tried to figure out which was better — to misbehave in third grade with girls my own age or to do well in a class older than me — I decided the second choice was the better one.

I've spent three months in the fourth grade. There are only two more months left to the school year. Yesterday, Mrs. Halevy asked me to come and speak with her.

"Listen to me, Sara," she said. "I am very pleased with what you have accomplished, and I think you are, too. Perhaps you would be willing to answer one question."

"Yes, I would," I heard myself answer agreeably.

"Why would a girl who was doing so poorly in the third grade become a top student in the fourth grade, all in the same year?"

"I can't figure it out myself!" I answered truthfully.

"Well, maybe I have the answer," said the teacher. "It's called willpower."

I had nothing to say.

"Sometimes life is hard, and I know your problem still hasn't gone away. But a person has to know how to keep on going in spite of her problems," said Mrs. Halevy, "and knowing how includes wanting to. Tomorrow, you will be going back to your own class and I'm sure you will put the same effort into your work there that you have put in here. You'll wind up doing just as well with them."

I was silent. I mean, on the one hand, I had been dying to go back to my own class. But now I suddenly had a choking feeling in my throat.

"Mrs. Halevy," I said finally.

She looked at me.

"I...I...I really..."

"Really?" she asked.

"Really!" I said, laughing.

"I'm glad," Mrs. Halevy smiled, and then she did something amazing. She got up and hugged me. "I am very happy," she said again. She patted me on the shoulder and waved goodbye.

"I really love you," I finally said out loud. But she was gone.

My Kid B(r)other

My name is Mordechai. I'm in the third grade and I do okay in school. I get along just fine with almost all the kids in my class. There's only one boy in the world that I cannot get along with — my brother Lazar.

Lazar's only in the first grade. He's a little kid, and he doesn't even know how to read and write very well. But, oh boy, he sure knows how to make me angry!

He always manages to find something that will annoy me. Maybe it'll be games of mine that he takes, or maybe my school notebook that he'll scribble on — something. And for no reason — just like that.

He doesn't bother my stuff because he needs it. He just wants to make me angry.

And then there's the way he can drive me crazy with a word. I can't explain exactly how he gets a single word to annoy me, but he does.

Sometimes he just repeats it over and over, again and again, maybe a thousand times, in order to see me explode.

Then other times he makes fun of me — imitates me or repeats everything I say. When he starts, I try not to pay attention. But when he keeps it up for a long time, I just can't control myself anymore.

That's when I give him a smack. And get one right back from my mother.

I always try to explain to my mother that she shouldn't punish me. I'm only giving Lazar what he deserves, because he's annoying me on purpose. But my mother keeps saying that I'm older and I should just ignore it, and anyway I certainly shouldn't punish him myself. I should tell her and she'll take care of the punishment.

I tried it her way a few times and I don't like what happens. Instead of *punishing* him, she usually just yells at him until he cries. I always think he's just pretending to cry, because why would someone cry if he didn't get a punishment or a smack?

Yesterday, he scribbled all over my pencil case. I slapped him. My mother got angry and said that she's the only one who's allowed to give punishments.

I was very upset. I tried to explain to her that I'm bigger than he is and I should have the right to punish him. I told her that I just can't stand the things he does anymore. I told her that if I don't train him to be a good kid, soon she's going to have one really rotten kid on her hands. I told my mother a lot of other things yesterday. I can't remember all of them.

I just remember that I cried. And hard, because I felt really hurt. I felt like I had been treated unfairly for an awfully long time.

My mother tried to calm me down, but she didn't have such an easy time. Finally she asked me, "Why do you think he acts this way?"

"Because he's bad," I answered. "He takes advantage of being little and getting your sympathy, and so he tortures me."

My mother looked at me and asked, "Do you really think he's a bad person?"

I nodded.

"Are you a bad person?"

"No!" I answered. "Of course I'm not. Ask any of my friends."

My mother said, "Wait one second." Then she went to the door of the room and called Goldie, my older sister, who's in the sixth grade.

"Goldie, do you remember what Moderchai used to do to you when he was little?"

"Of course I remember," she answered. "He was always bothering me, pulling my hair, scribbling in my notebooks, and whenever my girl-

friends came over, he wouldn't leave us alone for a minute."

I couldn't believe it. "Really?" I asked. "Are you sure that was me?"

Goldie went out and came back a few minutes later. She was holding an old binder. She opened it and a whole bunch of torn notebooks fell out.

"See these?" she said. "These are my third-grade notebooks. One day you went into my book bag and took them all out. After scribbling on each of them, you ripped every single one. You were in kindergarten."

I looked at them and I couldn't believe my eyes. I was so ashamed of myself for doing such a thing.

"So, what do you say, Mordechai? Are you a bad person?" asked my mother.

"No, I wouldn't say that. I think it's just that I was little and I didn't really understand what I was doing."

"Oh, so that's what you think? Well, in a few years, Lazar will say the very same thing. Try to be patient. When he's a little bigger he'll stop making so much trouble," my mother said.

So that's my story. I have a little brother who I don't get along with, but now I realize that it's just for now. In a few years, we'll get along fine — like I get along with Goldie. And Goldie and I really do get along great.

On Being Nice

My name is Tali. I'm in the fifth grade. My best friend is named Bracha. The two of us have always been in the same class. Our parents are friends, she lives next door to me, and we spend a lot of time at each other's houses. We even do our homework together.

Naturally, we always ask our teachers to let us sit next to each other. Since both of us are good students, and we don't disturb the class, the teachers let us.

This year, as always, we sat next to each other from the beginning. But then, about a month after school started, the teacher announced some changes. Before anyone could say a word of protest, I found Michal sitting next to me in the place where Bracha should have been.

Michal's a quiet girl — not the best student, not the worst. She lives in a neighborhood far

away from mine, and I never had anything much to do with her.

As soon as she sat down, I explained to her that I'm used to sitting next to Bracha, and asked if she could do me a favor and get the teacher to switch her seat with Bracha's again.

Michal told me straight out: she was not interested in switching. If I didn't want her next to me, I could go ask the teacher myself.

I went and the teacher refused. "I have my reasons," she said, and she pointed for me to go back to my seat.

"Well, I won't be nice to her," I mumbled.

The teacher gave me a sharp look. "What did you say?"

I didn't repeat it.

"Please sit down," the teacher commanded.

I sat down. But from that day on, I did not say a word to Michal. I didn't even look in her direction.

It wasn't long before the other girls in the class saw that I wasn't speaking to Michal. They started saying that Michal had "forced herself on Tali." I added fuel to the fire by repeating to everyone how much I didn't want to sit next to her. It made Michal unhappy, but she wouldn't ask the teacher to change her seat.

I wanted my best friend back. I was afraid that if I would be nice to Michal, then Bracha and I would stop being best friends, and I didn't want to lose her.

So, more than seven weeks passed, and I still didn't dare talk to Michal. Then one day I turned to wink at Bracha (something I'd do a couple of times during the day), and I froze. There was my best friend chatting with the girl next to her, Atara. They were even laughing!

That does it, I thought. Bracha doesn't want to be my best friend anymore. She likes Atara now. I felt so sad and alone.

After school, Bracha waited for me by the bulletin board like she usually did so we could walk home together. But I walked right past her without saying a word.

"Tali, wait up," she called after me. "What's wrong? Aren't we going home together?"

I didn't answer. I just kept going and walked home alone.

Bracha called my house a few times in the afternoon and a few more times at night, but I wouldn't come to the phone. "I'm sorry," my mother said to her, "but Bracha says she's not speaking to you."

The next day, when I glanced back at Bracha in class, there she was talking to Atara again. Well, if that's how she's going to be about it, I thought, I'm just going to talk to Michal.

I leaned over and said, "Hey, Michal, I'm

sorry. Can we just forget about it and start all over?"

Michal nodded yes and smiled.

That day after school, Bracha was waiting for me as usual. I walked right past her, my head held high.

"What is it with you?" she called after me. But I just kept on going.

The third day, whenever I saw Bracha speaking with Atara, I turned and found something to say to Michal. When I left school, Bracha saw me and blocked my path.

"You're going to have to tell me what's going on," she said, "or I won't let you go."

I was so angry, but really I was so hurt. "You're Atara's friend now and not mine," I blurted out, and then I began to cry.

"What are you talking about?" she asked. "*You're* my best friend, not her."

"But you talk to...her...so much in class," I said between my sobs.

"Sure I do," Bracha replied. "We sit next to each other, don't we? But just because I'm nice to her in class doesn't mean you're not my best friend. I've never played with her after school, and I don't even call her on the telephone."

"I thought you didn't want me anymore," I wailed.

"But you're my best friend," Bracha shouted

at me, and then we hugged and walked home together.

So in school, I decided to keep being nice to Michal and Bracha's still nice to Atara, but that doesn't change what we are to each other. We're best friends — before, during and after school.

My name is Mendy. I'm nine.

When I read "KIDS SPEAK", I felt like I really wanted to speak too. I have lots to say, but I dont know how.

The most right thing to say about me is that I love to play in the house, but most especially outside. I have lots of friends that are always looking for me. Especially the kinds of kids that are bored and want to find something to do.

These are my kinds of games: collecting scraps and junk from factories, finding rocks and pieces of cement so I can put together a fence around the building we live in. And I even once built a piece that slants from the sidewalk down into the street near our building so that it could be easy for me to go down off the curb with my bike.

My games always seem to get me awful dirty. And this makes my mother mad, and she also worries and she says that a normal boy souldn't have to get so dirty and he should play less and learn more. She always says to me: Mendy, what's gonna be with you? What will you do when you start learning Gemara? Enough playing!

Do you think my mother is right to be worried?

My name is Avi. I'm in the fifth grade.

About three years ago, I had to fly to <u>chutz la'Aretz</u>. It was terribly frosty cold there and snow was falling. I loved the snow for making snowmen— that was the good side. But the other side was that it was freezing, freezing cold there—40° below. It was so cold that a lot of things froze—even the tears that little kids cried froze on their faces. The water pipes and the sewer pipes froze. But one faucet didn't freeze, so we used it to wash <u>netilas yadayim</u>.

Yours, Avi

The Pilot

I'm Rafi and I'm in the fourth grade. I'm not such a hot student. In fact, until recently, I was a really weak one. I'm not dumb or anything like that. I just have a certain nature that keeps me from making progress in school.

You see, I'm a...pilot. Well, not really. But that's what they call me.

Lots of times in class I'll suddenly notice that all the kids are laughing. And then I'll realize that the teacher has been calling my name over and over, and I haven't heard him...because I've been lost in my dreams.

That's why they call me "the pilot." At times I just cut myself off from all that's going on around me and take off for somewhere. I imagine all sorts of things and lose myself in my thoughts. I'm just like a pilot who can take off and fly into the clouds, far away from all the people on the ground.

You may be surprised to hear it, but I'm not at all insulted by the nickname. I mean, first of all, "pilot" is not a very insulting title, it seems to me. And secondly, it describes the way I am. I really do separate myself from everyone else sometimes and fly off into my own world of thoughts, plans, and fantasies.

Want an example? Well, sometimes I imagine that I'm already twenty years old. I picture how I will look and how people will take me seriously. I picture the clothes I will wear, which yeshiva I'll learn in, and even little things like how my room will look at the yeshiva.

Then I go on to imagine the school that I'll be principal of when I'm grown. That's how I am.

The problem is that I don't dream these dreams while I'm asleep, but I do it right in the middle of the day during class.

I don't close my eyes, they tell me. I keep them open. I kind of stare at some point in the distance and away I go.

Then the kids around me will notice and say, "There he goes, he's off piloting somewhere." But I don't hear a word. I'm far, far away. Only when they actually shake me and say, "Hey, Rafi, wake up!" do I come back to earth. Sometimes I ask them how long I was "away."

My parents have been very worried about me lately. My father even took me once to some expert who was supposed to figure out whether or not I have a problem and how serious it is. She asked me all kinds of strange questions. At first, I answered all of them. But then I noticed a really nice picture on her wall with towers and castles...and I started imagining how I would build those things out of Lego. I'm really good at Lego — did I tell you?

Meanwhile, she kept asking her questions, and I answered her, but I have no idea what I said.

Afterwards, she told my father some things, which he's been telling me. He explained that I'm a very creative child, but that I have to try to control my thoughts, because I can't go on sitting in the classroom and also flying off into imaginary worlds at the same time.

So I've been working at it, and trying hard not to lose my head and fly off in the middle of class. I try to keep my flights for after school.

I have a trick that helps me do this. Every day, I set a length of time that I'm going to force myself to pay attention and not fly away. First, I made myself stay put for fifteen minutes. When I succeeded in staying on the ground for that amount of time, I added five minutes to it for the next day. And the next day another five, and so on.

At this point, I am able to keep my head for

fifty-five whole minutes in a row. Don't think it's easy. But it's a fact; I'm doing it.

I think that if I really try, I could become a good student. I think that I'm smart enough, besides being a pilot. Maybe I could fly up to the top of the class!

I Can Do It

My name is Mindy. I'm a fourth grader and not much of a student. In fact, I'm often called the class goof-off. I've heard it more than once, and each time it almost breaks my heart. I mean, I know I'm not an A-student or anything like that, but "class goof-off" — that's something else. Who wants to be called that?

I must admit, though, that it's not too far off. My handwriting, for example, is really scary. My mother says it looks like a collection of squiggles and lines. She says I'll make a good doctor, because no one can read their handwriting either. But that's not fair. I mean, *I* can read what I've written. But, I guess if no one else can, it's no good.

And my notebooks... They are usually a bunch of messy papers hanging from a crooked spiral wire. That's because I rip out a lot of pages in order to make paper airplanes or to draw pictures. Sometimes my notebooks fall on the floor and everyone steps on them and they get ripped. But that's not my fault, is it?

I also get bored in class. I mean, I don't pay attention much, and then I start daydreaming. When I snap out of it, I see that I've doodled stuff all over the cover of my notebook.

Other times I doze off for a minute with my head on my desk, and when I get up, I see I've wrinkled all my papers. So I'm not surprised that my notebooks look awful. That's just the way I am and that's how it is.

Homework — well, I guess my homework doesn't always get done. The truth is that I write down the questions, and I really do plan to answer them. But they get lost sometimes, and other times I just forget I have any homework.

You've probably noticed that I'm writing a lot of bad things about myself. And maybe you're asking yourself: "Isn't she embarrassed?"

Actually, I'm very embarrassed and I would never tell all this to anybody. But I don't mind writing about it to MORE KIDS SPEAK, because the readers won't know who I am. So it's kind of like writing to myself. But that's also not so easy, because I'm ashamed even in front of myself!

Two months have gone by since this school year started, and to tell the truth, I've pretty much given up on myself. But then a small ray of hope entered my life. I want to tell you about it here.

Two weeks ago my teacher started making trouble for me. What do I mean by "trouble"? It all started one day when my teacher took me into the teachers' lounge after class and announced, "From now on, Mindy, I am going to keep an eye on you."

At first I didn't know what she meant. But the very next day I found out. When the teacher came into the room and we all stood up, she looked at all of us one by one. Then her eyes stayed on me. She told us all to sit down and take out our *siddurim*, and then she motioned for me to come up to her desk.

"Go home and change your blouse, Mindy," she whispered to me when I was standing in front of her.

I was shocked. "But why?" I asked her.

She continued to speak quietly, "Because I can see your whole breakfast on it. You ate a tomato, bread with cheese, and...let me see — a sunny side up egg."

I was amazed. "How did you know that?" I asked.

"It's very simple," she answered and pointed to the front of my blouse. "Here are some leftover pieces of tomato, and here's a bit of cheese. This yellow on your sleeve must the yolk of your egg.

Well, am I right?"

I just had to laugh.

"Mindy, if you want to know why your work is so poor in school," she told me, "you have only to look at yourself in the mirror. You don't seem to care at all about your appearance. You don't mind if you and your clothes are all dirty. You don't even bother to look in the mirror. So it's no surprise that you're sloppy about your studies, as well.

"The richest businessman in the world," she continued, "will become poor very quickly if he fails to keep order in his books and accounts. And the smartest student will do poorly in school for the same reason.

"If you want to become a good student," she went on, "the first thing you must work on is keeping yourself and your books and papers clean and orderly. Do you want to be a good student, Mindy?" my teacher asked.

I nodded yes.

"Then you must work on keeping yourself and your school things clean and orderly. Let's start today. As soon as we finish *davening*, run home and change. Okay?"

The girls had been waiting all this time to start *davening*, so I ran to my seat and we began. Immediately afterwards I went home. My mother was so embarrassed when she heard why I had come back home.

"Why don't you listen to me when I tell you to watch how you eat? Now your teacher probably thinks I don't pay any attention to you!"

Well, that was just the beginning. From then on, the teacher kept after me about order and cleanliness. It mostly wasn't words she used, but gestures. She'd motion to me to tuck in my blouse or go wash my face. (My face seems to collect bits and pieces of my meals and assorted other things that don't belong there.)

Today the teacher got started on my textbooks and notebooks. She called me into the teachers' lounge and told me her plan.

"Look, Mindy," she began, "I'm not going to leave you alone. I can see that you're already doing much better. Why, just look at your blouse and skirt. Almost perfect. Was your chocolate at recess good? See, here's a smudge in the corner of your mouth. But that can happen to anyone. All in all, you have improved a great deal in taking care of your appearance. Now we will turn our attention to your notebooks."

She took my notebooks out of my book bag, and right in front of my eyes went through them page by page.

She didn't say a word. The notebooks said it all. Boy, was I embarrassed. A few times, when she came to a page that was clean and not torn or wrinkled, she wrote "excellent" at the top. I could see she was trying to find something good about my schoolwork, but it wasn't easy.

After she finished, she opened her own school bag and took out ten brand-new note-books. "Tomorrow, you will leave your old note-books at home," she told me. "You will cover these new ones nicely and start them fresh. Is that clear?"

I nodded.

The teacher got up to go, but first she put her hand on my shoulder. "You must believe that you can do it. That's all I ask," she said, and left.

Well, here I am writing this very late at night. As soon as I got home from school, I started covering each notebook neatly and carefully. My older sister helped me draw something pretty on the cover of each one. I even took off the messy old covers of my schoolbooks and put on new, clean ones. I'm sure that when I get to school tomorrow the teacher will have a good word for me.

Listen, it's not going to be easy to change so much. But if I don't try, it'll never happen.

Why Can't I Read?

My name is Gershon, and I'm in the fourth grade. But I still can't read or write very well! I'm not lazy, really I'm not. It's just the opposite: my teacher says I'm the best kid in the class.

So how come the best kid in the class can't read? Good question. Let me explain it to you. When we first learned *alef-beis*, I was great at calling out the letters with the other kids. But when the teacher asked me to go to the blackboard, I could never find the letter he wanted me to point out. And if my mother asked me to write an *alef*, it would come out backwards.

Lots of people thought something was wrong with me. Especially when we started writing and all my letters came out backwards. And boy, you should have heard me trying to read those words!

It wasn't until I got to the third grade that my parents finally realized I was smart in spite of this problem. They saw that I had memorized all of the *davening*. (I had to — I couldn't read my *siddur*.) And I also knew large sections of *Chumash* and even *Mishnah* by heart. They saw I had a good head... There were lots of things I was good at. I just couldn't read or write — that's all.

"How can this be?" my parents and my teachers used to ask me all the time. "You are so bright, and yet you can't read."

I didn't know why, myself. I knew I wasn't stupid, but I didn't know why I was having so much trouble.

Then my teacher invited my parents to come to his house and discuss me. A few days later, my parents took me to a woman who asked me a lot of questions and let me play all kinds of logic and memory games.

Afterwards, I heard her telling my parents, "He has a very high Intelligence Quotient — he's almost a genius."

Well, I knew what a genius was, but I didn't understand those other words she said. Then my mother explained that the woman had been giving me a special kind of test — called an IQ test for short — to see how smart I am. And I did very well on it!

"So how come I'm the only one in class who still can't read?" I asked.

"We're going to try to find that out next," promised my mother.

We went to a few more people who spoke nicely to me, and I liked them all. They seemed to understand me and my problem, and they looked like they really wanted to help. In the end, they were able to explain to my parents exactly what my problem was.

It's something called dyslexia. It's not easy for me to explain, but I'll try.

See, when you read these lines, your eyes have to report all the letters to your brain, right? Then your brain has to know which letter is which and put them together into words. Well, something happens somewhere between my eyes and my brain. Either the letters don't get to my brain right — some of them get mixed up with others or flip upside down — or a whole line can just get lost somewhere and mix me up. That's why I can't read.

Well, when I first heard this, it made me feel better. For sure I wasn't a dummy... It was more of a problem with my eyes than with my brain, right? But a little later I started to worry again, when I realized that this wasn't the kind of eye problem that glasses could fix. It did have more to do with my brain than I thought, and what on earth could fix that?

But then a special teacher started to show

me a different way of reading. It's too hard to explain here. Let me just say that I have to work really hard at it, and I use my memory a lot. Mostly I have to look at the letters not as letters, but as pictures. Think of a picture of an *alef*, let's say. Even if I see the picture upside down or slanty, I know that I have to read it as an *alef*. I also learned to recognize the shapes of thousands of words, and to remember what those words say. Now when I read, nobody can tell that I'm different from anyone else.

I also learned to write on a computer, which is so much easier for me because I don't have to look at the letters. Remember, my whole problem begins when I look at the letters.

I know, you probably don't understand my problem. Believe me, even I don't understand it that much. But I want to ask you kids a big favor.

If you ever have someone like me in your class, a kid who can't read or write, don't make fun of him, like some kids used to do to me. Don't think he's stupid. He just has a problem called dyslexia, and he can get over it, if only the right people will help him.

If you want to know who helped me the most, I'll tell you: It was my mother. She was patient with me, and spent a lot of time helping me. And now, because of her, I really am the best student in the class.

She says it's because of my own work. It's true — if I hadn't tried hard, I never would have gotten so far. But without her, I couldn't have done it either.

I really love her.

My Father's Tractor

My name is Dina. I'm in the third grade. If the name of this story made you think that my father owns a tractor, then I fooled you. My father doesn't have a tractor. He doesn't even know how to drive one. My father owns a store, and he works really hard in it from morning till night.

My father is a very special man. He helps everybody, and he's really nice to each person who comes into his store. He's also very nice to me.

So what does all this have to do with a tractor?

I'll tell you, but only if you promise not to laugh at this story, even if it sounds strange to you.

A long time ago, when I was really little, I asked my father to tell me a story at bedtime — like all kids ask.

My father thought and thought. Then he said, "I'm sorry, Dina, but I can't seem to think of a story to tell you. I'm no story writer — I just work in a store."

"But fathers have to tell stories to their children. Please," I insisted.

My father sighed. "Let me think some more."

He thought and thought for a while. "Believe me, little Dina, I don't know how to tell stories. Maybe you'll let me read you one from a book."

"Oh, come on, Abba," I begged. "I know all those stories already. Tell me a story of your own."

So my father thought some more. Then he cleared his throat and he began to tell me the strangest story I had ever heard in my whole life.

"Once upon a time there was a tractor that loved to help children. One day the tractor met a little boy named Matty. Matty was crying. He explained to the tractor that he didn't know how to read and that it made him very sad. The tractor discussed the problem with the hoopoe bird, and she flew off to Matty's school. There she told all the children in first grade that if they helped Matty learn to read they would get a free ride on the tractor."

"What happened in the end?" I asked.

"The end was that they helped Matty and

he learned how to read. Not all of the children helped Matty, but most of them did. And everyone that helped Matty flew on the hoopoe's wings all the way to the tractor and got the ride that was promised to them."

I kept quiet.

"Did you like the story?" asked my father.

"What's a hoopoe?" I asked.

"A hoopoe is a kind of bird," he said.

"And who was driving the tractor?" I asked.

"Oh, the tractor knew how to drive all by itself," my father said. But he couldn't explain exactly how.

"So, was it a good story?" my father asked me again.

"No," I answered. "It was silly. It didn't make any sense."

"Well, I told you I don't know any good stories," my father said and he kissed me good night. I thought he looked a little sad.

The next night I asked my father again to tell me a story.

He began, "Once upon a time there was a tractor that had a fight with a hoopoe bird. They didn't speak to each other for a long time. Then Matty came along and told the tractor that the hoopoe was very sad. The other children also tried to make peace between them. In the end, they made up, and decided never to fight again."

I kept quiet.

"Did you enjoy the story, Dina?" my father asked me.

"No," I said. "Tractors don't fight. And for sure not with hoopoes."

My father said good night and left.

This went on for weeks, even months. Every night, my father would tell me a story. It always began with the words, "Once upon a time there was a tractor."

Then I started first grade and I learned how to read on my own. I would look at a book every night. But just before bedtime, my father would come to me and tell the usual story about that tractor, the hoopoe, and Matty. In time, they were joined by Yochanan the fisherman, Shemuel the carpenter, and tons of children, teddy bears, and trucks.

It was at the beginning of second grade that my father stopped telling me bedtime stories and I stopped asking for them. I guess he thought I was too big to hear about that silly tractor anymore. He also knew that I had started reading stories on my own. I really do read lots and lots of stories now.

About a year and a half ago, my baby brother Menachem was born. I love him so much. He was born after a lot of years without any baby brothers or sisters.

Last night, Menachem started to cry after everyone was already asleep. He wouldn't stop crying. Both my parents woke up, and so did I, because Menachem sleeps in my room.

My father got out of bed and came into our room. I saw how tired he was by the way he was walking. My father works really hard — but I said that already.

I made believe I was asleep. I peeked a little to see how my father would get Menachem to be quiet.

My father picked Menachem up in his arms and started to rock him. But Menachem kept crying. He put him back down on his stomach, but he screamed.

Then he picked him up again, and he said softly, near Menachem's ear, "Once upon a time, there was a tractor that met a hoopoe bird that was always crying." Menachem suddenly stopped crying.

"The tractor said to her, 'Why are you crying, hoopoe?' and she answered, 'Because Matty's parents have no fish for Shabbos.'"

Menachem looked at my father with interest, even though I don't think he understood a word.

I smiled under my blanket. I had a feeling this was a new beginning for the tractor and the hoopoe, and that we'd have a story every night, maybe until Menachem would be seven...

"And, as soon as the tractor gave Matty's parents the fish that Yochanan the fisherman had caught, the hoopoe was happy and she stopped her crying." My father smiled as he finished the story, which I knew by heart.

Then my father said, "Menachem, did you like the story?" But Menachem didn't answer. He was asleep.

Suddenly I found myself answering, "I liked the story very much, Abba."

My father turned toward my bed. "Dina, you're awake?"

"Yes," I smiled at him.

"Did you really like the story?" he asked.

"Really."

"But it doesn't make any sense," my father reminded me.

"I know," I said. "But...I've been missing those stories for a long time. I've sort of been waiting for the day when you'd start to tell them again. I know they don't make sense, but..."

"Well, love doesn't make any sense either," said my father. "You asked me for stories and all I had was love. But you wanted a story, so I did my best for you. Do you understand?"

"I understood a long time ago," I said, and I got up to hug my father.

Friends Who Argue

My name's Aryeh, and I'm in the sixth grade. I have a good friend named Eliyahu. The two of us live right near each other and we always walk to school together and come home together.

We're very different from one another. Eliyahu's very tall, and I'm short. He has dark hair and mine's light.

Our personalities are totally different, too. Eliyahu says very little, and I'm a real talker. Eliyahu's very reserved. You'll never hear him yelling or laughing loudly. Everything he does is very measured. Me, I know how to scream, how to laugh out loud, and even how to cry.

There's an ongoing argument between the two of us about how people should behave. Eliyahu says that a person shouldn't show all his feelings. He thinks that a kid who laughs

out loud or cries in front of others is like a baby.
According to Eliyahu, the whole world doesn't
have to know how you feel about everything. If
you're happy — you don't have to go wild, and if
you're sad — you don't have to show it in front
of everyone.

Now take me. I have the exact opposite opinion. I believe a normal kid, when he's happy,
should show his happiness to the world. When
he's sad, he should feel free to tell people how
he feels. And when he's tense, he has to be able
to release that tension (in a way that's okay, of
course. He can't go around smashing things or
anything.)

In short, I really think that a kid should
express what he feels and not keep his feelings
hidden inside. But this argument will never end.
We've gotten used to the fact that we will always
disagree about it.

And don't think that it's only about this that
we disagree. The fact of the matter is that we
argue all day long, about every subject in the
world. We argue on our way to school, on the
way home from school, and during recess. It's
a rule — we almost never agree with each other
about anything.

For example, when Eliyahu said a certain
gemara was hard, I insisted that it was really
simple, and how could he think it was hard?

And when I said that a *Chumash* test was hard, Eliyahu said I probably hadn't studied enough, because it really was quite easy. And each time it turned into a roaring argument, with each of us bringing reasons why he was right and the other was wrong.

What's interesting about us is that, in spite of our constant arguing, we have always stayed very close. We've been best friends since the first grade.

One day we were walking home from school together as usual. For some crazy reason, after all these years, we started an argument about which way home was shorter.

I claimed that it was faster to walk through the park. Eliyahu said that it was faster to walk down Clark Street. Well, we stood at the intersection of Clark and Vine, and neither one of us would give in and walk the way the other preferred. After arguing for a really long time, we parted in anger and each of us went our separate way.

Well, for a number of days we did the same, silly thing. We would walk together for only the first block, until that intersection, and then we would separate.

The truth was that I regretted the whole thing. I was bored walking home by myself. But there was no way I would give in to Eliyahu.

A week passed, and I decided I couldn't go on like this. I went to Eliyahu and I said, kind of casually, "Hey listen, maybe we could take turns — one day we'll go your way and one day we'll go my way?"

Eliyahu agreed immediately and offered to go my way the first day. As we walked, Eliyahu admitted that he hadn't known what to do — he had also regretted what had happened.

"Really?" I asked.

"Didn't you see that I was sad?" he asked.

"No," I answered. "You know how you keep your feelings inside."

He didn't answer, so I pressed my point. "If I hadn't come over to you, you would never have come over to me, right? You would have just stayed sad for ages and ages, and kept it inside. But I — as soon as I decided that I didn't like to walk alone — I came right over and told you. So which is better, keeping it in or being open like me?"

I ended on a note of victory; I was sure I had won the argument at last. But, of course, this was the perfect chance for us to start the whole disagreement over again. We actually sank into it happily.

It's years since we started walking together. We still argue constantly. We're still amazingly different. It's usually I who starts by attacking

Eliyahu's opinion and personality. But do you know what? I think I never had such a good friend. The fact that he can argue so strongly and still stay friendly shows the special kind of stuff he's made of.

But don't tell him I said so.

Glossary

The following glossary provides a partial explanation of some of the Hebrew, Yiddish, and Aramaic words and phrases used in this book. The spellings and explanations reflect the way the specific word is used herein. Often, there are alternate spellings and meanings for the words.

ABBA: daddy.

ALEF-BEIS: the Hebrew alphabet.

ALIYOS: the sub-divisions of the weekly Torah reading, for each of which another member of the congregation is called up to recite the blessings.

ARON KODESH: the Holy Ark where the Torah scrolls are stored in the synagogue.

ASHREI YOSHVEI VEISECHA: "Happy are those who dwell in Your house," the opening words of the first prayer in the MINCHAH service.

AVERAH: a sin.

BARUCH HASHEM: "Thank God!"

BEIS KNESSES: a synagogue.

BIMAH: a dais; the raised platform in the synagogue where the leader of the services stands.

BITACHON: trust in God.

CHAZAN: the leader of the prayer service.

CHUMASH: [one of the five volumes of] the Torah.

DAVEN: (Y.) to pray.

FRUM: (Y.) religious.

GEMARA: commentary on the MISHNAH; together they comprise the Talmud.

IMMA: mommy.

KIPPAH: a yarmulka.

MA'ARIV: the evening prayer service.

MIDDOS: character traits.

MINCHAH: the afternoon prayer service.

MINYAN(IM): a quorum of ten adult males, required for public prayer services.

MISHNAH (-NAYOS): the oral Law, codified by R. Yehudah Ha-Nasi (chapters of the Oral Law).

NACHAS: pleasure; joy.

NETILAS YADAYIM: the ritual hand-washing before eating bread or upon arising, or on other required occasions.

SHAMAYIM: Heaven.

SHTENDER: (Y.) a book stand; a lectern.

SIDDUR(IM): prayer book(s).

SIYYUM: [a party celebrating] the completion of the study of a volume of MISHNAYOS or a tractate of GEMARA.

SOFER: a [Torah] scribe.

TEHILLIM: [the Book of] Psalms.

TESHUVAH: atonement.

YETZER HA-RA: the evil inclination in human nature.